Other Books by Dr. Nowell

Reluctant Millionaires

CTR: Critical Thinking Rules

Books in Progress-Coming Sooner & Later

The Laws of Happiness

Addiction Elimination

Change Your Program to Change Your Life

Two-Face "Secrets" (Series)

All About Liars

Lifestyle Enhancement

Understanding & Helping Your Adolescent

Anger Elimination

This book is about how you learn anger, why you do anger, and how to get rid of your anger forever.

By

Brian L. Nowell, Ph.D.

The Development Center Publishing
Sioux Falls, South Dakota

Dedication:

To my Father, who is always there for me, to help me become a better man of good character, to help me become a better son, brother, husband, and father, and to help me become a dedicated helper of the poor and needy.

Acknowledgements: I am very grateful for help and the constructive criticism that my family members and friends have generously given, as I have worked to produce this book for you. I let my feeling get hurt and resisted needed changes at times, but fortunately I got over that and made the needed changes. To you generous helpers, thanks to each of you.

Copyright:

© Brian L. Nowell & THE DEVELOPMENT CENTER 2009, 2016 ALL RIGHTS RESERVED.

No part of this book may be reproduced, stored in a retrieval system, or transmitted, in any form, for any reason, or by any means, electronic, mechanical, photocopying, recording, or otherwise, without the prior written permission of the Managing Director of the Development Center and the author Brian L. Nowell, Ph.D.

You are strongly encouraged to take full responsibility for all of your thoughts, emotions, and behaviors.

This publication is designed to provide accurate and authoritative information in regard to the subject matter covered. It is sold with the understanding that the author, the copyright holder, and the publisher are not engaged in rendering counseling, therapy, psychotherapy, or any other related therapeutic professional services. If you believe that any of those services or any other such expert assistance is required, the services of a competent and caring professional person should be sought.

Brian L. Nowell and The Development Center Educational Disclaimer:

I, Brian L. Nowell, am a developmental psychologist and an educator, not a psychological therapist. I do not have any therapy services for sale. You will do or not do the things that I discuss in this book at your own discretion; therefore you need to do your own thinking and research about anger elimination, and if desired for any reason, rely on your own psychological professionals to help you make your own effective decisions about applying anger elimination to your life. I and The Development Center do have the right and the obligation to present educational information about various things relating to anger elimination and about what I am personally doing about anger elimination.

ISBN 978-0-9713654-4-5

Printed in the United States of America
16 15 14 13 12 11 10 9 8 7 6 5 4 3

INTRODUCTION

I am an anger expert.

First of all, although I am not happy to admit it, I am an anger expert, because I have spent most of my life practicing and refining my anger habits. Second, and gratefully, I am an anger expert, because I have learned how to successfully eliminate anger from my own life and how to help anyone else who wants to get rid of his or her anger habits. I am also grateful to say that in addition to learning how to eliminate anger, I have learned many other very useful things about how to improve human happiness through my training and my wonderful experiences as a person, developmental psychologist, author, and educator.

In this book, I have included various true stories about my own and others' anger issues and unfortunate anger experiences. My main reasons for including these stories is to illustrate for you, in a personal way, the actual situations that stimulate us to get angry and the very real costs of anger in terms of abiding unhappiness, heightened stress, loss of productive time, and diminished relationship quality.

The stories that I have included are not happy stories, but they will certainly help you better understand anger and why the thoughts, feelings, and behaviors of anger are worth eliminating, if you want to increase success and happiness in your own life and in the lives of your friends and loved ones.

As I mentioned before, during my life, I have come to understand many important concepts that are vital for human happiness. In addition to learning those things, I have been and continue to be someone who applies what I have learned in my own life and in the lives of others.

I know that happiness is the result of living our lives in a state that is increasingly more positive and that includes choosing and continuing to develop more positive thoughts, beliefs, emotions, and behaviors. I have personally learned how to eliminate anger in my own life, thus producing greater personal and relationship happiness.

I have also learned precisely how to teach others, some of whom are much like you, to change their own emotional habits to increase their own happiness and strengthen their personal relationships. And I am confident that I can effectively teach you these things too.

Not too long ago I made a commitment to my father that I would share what I have learned about eliminating anger with as many people as possible. That is why I have written this book. It contains many important truths and the most important happiness producing emotional breakthrough that I have learned in the past 15 years. And when you learn, and then apply, these simple concepts in your life, you will realize exactly what I mean.

Then, when your life has changed for the better because you have applied what you have learned in this book, I sincerely hope that you will share what you have learned from me, with the people that you associate with and/or love.

Brian L. Nowell, Ph.D.
Positive/Developmental Psychologist

A Very Human, Developmental Work In Progress

TABLE OF CONTENTS

Preface	Program, Personality, & Emotional Intelligence	
Chapter 1	What "Gets Up Your Nose"	1
Chapter 2	Anger Habits	14
Chapter 3	Brian's Anger Issues	17
Chapter 4	Takers, Balancers, & Givers	26
Chapter 5	Justice or "Balancing The Scales"	34
Chapter 6	The Great & Dreadful Anger Path	38
Chapter 7	Reducing Anger By Replacing Anger Habits	47
Chapter 8	Reducing Anger: David's Story	57
Chapter 9	My Promise to My Wife	62
Chapter 10	Social Intuition & True Intuition/Insight	69
Chapter 11	Andy's Anger At Work	77
Chapter 12	Thoughts & Beliefs "Create" Emotions	84
Chapter 13	The Four Sources of Thoughts	89
Chapter 14	Anger Cities	97
Chapter 15	Gender & Other Anger Differences	104
Chapter 16	Ellen's Anger At Graduate School	117
Chapter 17	Hot Type A Equals Premature Death	125
Chapter 18	Roger's Anger Over The Years	131
Chapter 19	Why Anger Is Not Necessary	144
Chapter 20	My Most Important Insight About Anger	146
Appendix A	12 More Anger Stories	155

Preface

Throughout this book I use certain words from the English language in ways that may be easily misunderstood, because I use them in ways that are not usual. So, to hopefully prevent some misunderstanding, I have given a few brief explanations of some very important words for concepts that I often refer to or know to be foundational.

Program (Programming): Each of us has the ability to turn our choices of thoughts, emotions, and behaviors into automated habits that we do not have to think about in order for us to do them. We seem to have an infinite ability to do this, and that is a good thing. This is in the broadest sense our unconscious memories.

If we had to think consciously about anything that we did or prevented ourselves from doing, we would be virtually paralyzed mentally, emotionally, and physically. To get a sense of this, consider for a few moments the exceedingly complex process of muscle alterations in almost every part of a person's body, that are required for that person to successfully take a single balanced step.

When I write about our automatic mental, emotional, and/or behavioral reactions to the multitudes of physical, abstract, situational, and relationship matters in our lives, I refer to that as the operations of our program, our habits, our automated reactions, being on autopilot, our unconscious reactions, or our unconscious memories. I mean the same basic things when I use any of these words or phrases.

Personality: There are many disagreements, and in some cases a meaningful lack of clarity of understanding among psychological professionals, about what exactly a person's personality is, how it begins, and how it is altered. For my purposes in this book, I consider personality to be something that each of us is born with. As we gain control of our bodies in our infancy, we soon become able to express our personalities in quite complex ways.

Our personalities are very stable, such that they provide an ongoing foundation and structure that colors all of the rest of our lives, how we translate our experiences, how we relate to others, what we are attracted to and repelled by, and which define all of our strengths and weaknesses.

Part of how I think about and understand personality is in relation to what is known as the Big 5 (NEO) personality dimensions/factors and each of their 6 subscales/facets. These are as follows.
- Conscientiousness (competence, order, dutifulness, achievement striving, self-discipline, deliberation)
- Agreeableness (trust, straightforwardness, altruism, compliance, modesty, tendermindedness)
- Neuroticism (anxiety, hostility, depression, self-consciousness, impulsiveness, vulnerability to stress)
- Openness to Experience (fantasy, aesthetics, feelings, actions, ideas, values)
- Extraversion (warmth, gregariousness, assertiveness, activity, excitement seeking, positive emotion)

Each of us can fairly accurately describe and understand our basic nature and current strengths and weaknesses by getting a good understanding of what each of the subscales/facets represent in real life. And then, when we have that understanding, we can evaluate or rank ourselves for each subscale/facet on a scale of 1-10 (with 1 being the weakest or lowest amount and 10 being the strongest or greatest amount).

The dimension of Neuroticism is where anger resides. And the very good news is that personality is gradually changeable, by doing what is needed to change it. I will have much more to say about this later.

Emotional Intelligence: This is composed of a set of emotional abilities. Almost all of us are born with a full set of these, but for each of us, each of the following set of emotional abilities is at its own level of development.
- Feeling our own and others' emotions
- Describing our emotions accurately to self and others
- Telling others about emotions and what they mean
- Recognizing the honesty or dishonesty of our own and others emotions
- Maintaining conscious awareness of our own and others emotions over time
- Learning from our own emotional experiences and observations of others' emotional experiences
- Identifying emotion in pictures, faces, art, music, scenarios, and literature
- Being influenced by others emotions
- Effectively use our emotions to influence others thinking, attitudes, beliefs, and behaviors
- Choosing to feel or not feel, express or not express any emotion and how much of it.

Chapter 1

What "Gets Up Your Nose"

Universal Anger Stimulants or "Triggers"

While I was living in Germany in 2006, I met John, who had been a career police officer in the UK before moving to Germany to be near his children and grandchildren. We stared doing volunteer service work together, and soon became good friends and enjoyed some meaningful experiences together.

It was always fun for me, talking with John about his personal life and work experiences, and about life in the UK in general. Once when I was talking with John about anger, he delighted me by stating "What gets up my nose is…", which is a colloquialism that is common in the UK, and which as you see I have chosen as the title for this Chapter. What "gets up your nose" has to do with your **Core Emotional Issues**, which are the things that "make" you angry.

Each of us has one or more **Core Emotional Issues** that stimulate or trigger our anger habits. These core emotional issues are about things that are the most emotionally important to us as individuals. Our core emotional issues are about the presence or absence the specific and general sensations, communications, situations, actions, relationships, and/or events that trigger our thoughts, feelings, and behaviors of anger. Although each of us has our own, hopefully smaller, "favorite" set of core emotional issues, the list of core emotional issues in this Chapter is pretty comprehensive, with some overlap for some of the issues.

So, following is a list of 20 "popular" **Core Emotional Issues** that people commonly get angry about. In many cases, like in the true anger stories that are presented in this book, more than one core emotional issue often gets violated in any given anger event or situation. And, the more important the relationship, event, or situation is to us, the more likely that anger will result from a core emotional issues violation.

Core Emotional Issues that Stimulate or Trigger Anger

1. A personal moral or ethical trait, attribute, or strength being questioned or not believed

Many of us are very emotionally sensitive about certain of our moral or ethical attributes or strengths such as honesty, respect for others, conscientiousness, kindness, helpfulness, timeliness, etc. When these attributes or strengths are questioned or not believed by someone, it can very easily trigger our anger. In some cases this is because an individual wants to replace, or has recently replaced, the negative opposite of the positive attribute. The negative opposite is a weakness or moral/ethical failing, and so, for a recent change the individual is still emotionally sensitive about it.

2. Being used, tricked, lied to, or deceived by someone

Examples of this include being the victim of fraud, scheming, or dishonesty. There are many different types of this interpersonal problem, often coming from people that we don't know well, but may have to interact with, such as dishonesty by cab drivers, repair workers, insurance agents, automobile and other sales workers, etc. And, of course we can and at times do get victimized in these ways by those that we work with, those that we associate with, those that are our friends or family, and those that we love.

3. Disrespect toward you, a friend, or loved one

Everyone needs to be respected. To be disrespected is to be partially devalued, or to be thought of as inferior at least in some small way. It especially hurts to be thought of as inferior by someone whose opinion we value. And if we see a friend or loved one disrespected, we naturally become angry in their defense.

Disrespect is also manifested in rudeness and in being inappropriately ignored or dismissed.

4. Being strongly devalued by someone

There are many ways to be devalued. If you have ever been disrespected, that is a mild dose of being devalued. Being devalued also means to be thought of as being unimportant.

When I was attending graduate school, I once witnessed the custodian of a certain church building, who was also a graduate student, share his thoughtful religious ideas with the two religious leaders who taught at the building. When he did that, something happened that he did not expect. The two religious leaders minimized his ideas, and treated him as an inferior, probably because he was working as the "lowly" custodian.

I have also witnessed and heard accounts of men and women being devalued by their spouses, who thought themselves to be better than the spouses who were devalued. This was at times in the form of a spouse devaluing his/her partner because he/she was perceived to be not as skilled in parenting, budgeting, communicating, cleaning, or career advancement. (Chapter 18: Roger's Anger Over The years).

And finally, I have observed some of my professor peers, because of their prejudice against religion, subtly mock and devalue a few of their class members and/or faculty peers who are knowledgeable and faithful religionists in addition to being competent students or scholars.

It is probably true that honorable people worldwide who quietly and honestly live their good religious, moral, or spiritual beliefs and who do not devalue other people are devalued by some people around them who do not like or agree with their religious or spiritual beliefs. There are many ways to be devalued, and I have only included a few. Being devalued by those who believe themselves to be superior is highly offensive and, in many cases, leads to anger for the victim/target of the devaluing.

5. Prejudice and Discrimination

When someone is prejudiced about us, it generally means that he or she wrongfully believes that we are inferior to him or her in some important way, or in several important ways, because we are a member of some group that is devalued by her or him. Discrimination generally means being treated in a way that is inferior to the way that other people are treated because of something that is different about us, and that is believed to be inferior by the person who is discriminating.

This happens for many different reasons including, but not limited to, age, gender, weight, race, beliefs, or religion. I have personally observed and experienced prejudice and discrimination for each of these reasons, both privately and in work settings. In those instances, the greater the importance to me, of what was at "risk", because of the prejudice and/or discrimination, the more likely that I got angry about it.

6. Violation of Trust

I generally prefer to trust people or give them the benefit of the doubt, rather than to mistrust them initially. Before I learned to accurately assess individual amounts of trustworthiness, I made a lot of mistakes in terms of trusting people more than they were mature enough to fulfill. And, those violations of my trust most often led to my anger. The more important a person or situation is to us the more likely that a violation of our trust by them will lead to anger.

7. Abuse of Authority or Power

Being oppressed, being hindered, or being made to feel diminished by those in authority can trigger our anger. I was taught, many years ago, that most people, when they are given a little authority or power that affects other people, they tend to abuse that authority or power. Since then, I have consistently observed that this is certainly true.

I suppose that abuse of authority or power happens because those individuals who do it, have little other power or control in their lives, or that they have saved up a lot of bad emotions from being controlled or abused by others themselves. Abuse of authority or power is also frequently related to a person's low self esteem. That is, he or she tries to "elevate" himself/herself, by improperly hindering, controlling, opposing, or diminishing others.

8. Broken Promises

Broken promises occur in buying and selling transactions, in business dealings, in work relationships, in personal friend and love relationships, and in family interactions. Anger over broken promises is often learned early in life when parents do not keep their promises to their children. The acutest anger over broken promises occurs in love and spousal relationships because those relationships are the most important to us.

9. Being physically, verbally, financially, sexually, or emotionally abused, bullied or cheated

Probably many of us were abused or bullied in some way when we were children. And so, that sets us up to get angry about it from the many and often more subtle forms of abuse or "bullying" that we encounter as adults.

As children, many of us may have been bullied or abused by our siblings, relatives, school bullies, or even our teachers or parents. As adults, many of us may have been bullied or abused in some way by supervisors, bosses, or others who have some power or authority over us.

As for financial bullying, if we have ever bought or sold something like a car or some other important item, to someone much more experienced in buying and/or selling than we are, we may well have been financially abused by them in that buying or selling process. And certainly, there are many of us who have felt financially abused by the steadily increasing fees and taxes that we are required or compelled to pay.

If any of these things are so, we then have gotten pre-programmed to get angry about abuse, in the many and often more subtle forms that we encounter throughout our adult life.

10. A friend, a loved one, a helpless person, or an innocent person being threatened, harmed, or abused

Our natural protective instincts can lead us to anger. Would you get angry if your child's teacher punished her for smiling too much? What if your child's coach humiliated him in front of his teammates for some sports mistake, or if a relative of yours was accused, indicted, or convicted for a crime that she or he did not commit?

What if your child was harshly treated by a truant officer, a teacher or some other school authority for something someone else had done? What if a friend or loved one was repeatedly and cruelly sexually, emotionally, or physically abused by someone?

What if a driver seriously threatened or harmed your family members from reckless or DUI driving? What if you discovered that the spouse of your sibling or child was committing adultery? What if politicians of any political party lie, conceal, and deceive, just to get elected, and thus

Chapter 1: What "Gets Up Your Nose" 9

hurt the citizens that they are supposed to protect and prosper? Would you get angry about any of these things?

11. Property Issues--your property being carelessly damaged or lost or being purposefully damaged or stolen

Have you ever trusted someone to buy something for you, do something for you, or care for something that you value, and that person did a bad job of it? Have you ever let someone use something that you valued, and he or she damaged it? Have you ever had something valuable stolen from you or damaged by a vandal? If you have had any of these experiences, was anger the result?

12. Being denied something that is very important to you

Have you ever been fired or laid off from your employment? Been denied a loan for something that you really needed, even though you really would have been able to pay the loan back? Tried to get a desirable job, but not been hired? Applied to a school, but not been accepted? Tried to start a romantic relationship, but been spurned? Competed with your peers or a rival for what you believed was vital for you to have in terms of a relationship, an achievement, or a recognition, but your peer or rival got it instead of you? Tried to win an important game, but lost it? If any of this happened to you, were you angry?

13. Someone wrongfully taking credit for your plan, idea, work, or achievement

This occurs in many different types of organizations when someone selfishly steals the work and ideas of another (Chapter 4: Takers, Balancers, and Givers). Sadly, and although most of us do not know the true details about these things, this has happened with many of the notable inventions of our modern world. And, unfortunately, many supervisors/bosses/officers have wrongfully take credit for their subordinates plan, work, and achievements. Would you get angry if this kind of taking happened to you?

14. Personal failure in something that is very important to you

This is something that happens to almost all of us at some point in our lives. Here are two main examples of this. One involved a graduate student who was rejected for admission to the doctoral program of his desires. He became very angry (at those who denied his admittance) was bitter, and was otherwise unhappy for as long as I still knew about him.

The second example involved a man who was trying to learn about stock market trading, but just could not master it enough to be successful at that time. Although he was not wealthy or even particularly well off financially, over the course of several years he lost about $250,000 of his own hard earned money, and probably an amount equal to that of other's money (associate's and family member's) that they had entrusted to his care. Because he had a good moral foundation, this was a dreadful strain on him, and he was distressed and exceedingly angry (at himself) about it for much of the time, and for several years.

15. Dishonoring, opposing, or ignoring of requests, guidance, or instructions given to a subordinate or one's children, and the same neglect or opposition from one's spouse or coworker, when fulfillment of the requests, guidance, or instructions is appropriate

The effects of dishonoring, ignoring, and neglect of requests and instructions seem to be much worse in the close relationships of family than in the hierarchy of work relationships, and can result in a great deal of family sadness, upset, and anger.

16. Passive or active "sabotage", delay, or blockage, by someone, of an idea, a solution, an objective, a task, a communication, or a project that is important to you

I have seen this core emotional issue violated in social settings, in volunteer settings, in family settings, in friendships, and in work settings. Anger often feeds very well on this.

17. Anything that you consider to be meaningfully unjust or unfair

This is a broad type of core emotional issue. There are exceedingly many types of unfairness in the world every day, and most of them generate anger in people who believe in and want fairness. There are also very many things in our lives that we think or believe are unfair, which are really not so. Of course those things trigger anger too.

18. Anything (other than a person) that frustrates, hinders, or blocks something important to you

These things usually trigger anger in individuals who have a high personal need for control, and who often has many important things in his or her life out of control, or who has serious time pressures. Please see Chapter 18, Roger's Anger Over The Years, for prime examples of this anger stimulant.

19. Abuse of your time

Unfortunately, there are many people in the world who are selfish abusers of others' precious time. This time abuse can occur in a variety of both obvious and subtle ways. Chapter 4 about Takers, Balancers, and Givers will provide a better understanding of this.

20. Someone identifying, pointing out, or telling you about your <u>true</u> faults, weaknesses, failings, wrong behaviors, etc.

For most of us, having this done to us, even if it is done with well meaning intentions, is often deeply emotionally painful. So, as an emotional defense, many of us get angry when this happens to us, especially when it is repeatedly done by someone we care about. (Reading about the Anger Habit Path in Chapter 6 will give you a better

Chapter 1: What "Gets Up Your Nose"

understanding of the internal anger creating process involved).

It is our individual personalities combined with our life experiences that determine what will be a specific Core Emotional Issue for each of us. This process happens mostly out of our conscious awareness and programs our anger.

Often there are times when more than one of our core emotional issues is involved in a given life situation. When one or more core emotional issues are violated, almost all of us get angry about the event or situation, immediately and automatically. And, the more important the relationship, event, or situation, the more likely it is that we will react with anger as a result of the violations.

In the following chapters, I have included true anger stories to illustrate most of the universal anger stimulators listed above. Each situation that I share with you was costly to the participants in some way. It diminished their better humanity and needlessly harmed the others involved in the situations. Although the stories are true, I have changed the names, genders, and some details about the individuals involved to respect their privacy. As you read the stories in the following chapters, you may find that some or even all of the anger stimulants will be very familiar to you, either because you have personally experienced them for yourself or because you have observed similar situations and their anger results in others.

The following chapter explores anger as a habit.

Chapter 2

Anger Habits

Our Angers Are Habits That We Form By Choices That We Make, Mostly Out Of Our Conscious Awareness

The reason that we react immediately with anger when we are insulted or when we feel that something is unfair (Violations of our Core Emotional Issues), is that we have, without realizing it, automated our emotional response to the offensive event or situation. That means that we do not have to consciously think about how to respond to the offense or injustice. So, for that particular offense or injustice, we have formed a habit of reacting immediately with the emotion of anger.

Anger habits are potentially formed at many points of our lives and are all formed the same basic way. Please, consider the following simplified set of steps:

Chapter 2: Anger Habits   15

The Very Quick Path to Create Anger in 8 Basic Steps

1) An "event" occurs. An "event" represents the presence of some negative or the absence of some positive specific and general emotions, behaviors, words, sensations, situations, communications, actions, attitudes, relationships, etc.

2) You are consciously aware of the event. It may be near or far away.

3) You already care about the event or you choose to care about the event (you decide that it is emotionally important to you). You probably do not realize that you are doing this.

4) You already believe or you choose to believe that what has happened (a negative) or failed to happen (a desired positive) is unfair or personally offensive to you or someone else and that it harms or will harm you or the other person in some way, etc.

5) You experience emotional pain as a natural consequence because of your offended belief.

6) You do not like feeling that emotional pain and have a strong unconscious desire to eliminate is as soon as possible.

7) You unconsciously mentally change the emotional feeling of pain to the emotion feeling of anger by mentally re-labeling it as anger. We do this relabeling because we can, and the resulting anger serves a useful purpose to some degree, in that the anger emotion motivates us internally

and/or externally to try to restore "justice" or correct the wrong done to us.

8) You are motivated and energized to do something internally (in Thoughts and/or beliefs) and/or overtly (in your words or behaviors) about the injustice or offense.

This Anger Path process forms a very strong bond in you between the event and your anger. If the offense or your emotional pain is strong enough, your anger reaction habit is created from only one occurrence of the unjust or offensive event. However, even with less severe emotional pain/anger, a few repetitions of this Anger Path pattern are enough for your anger reaction habit to form strongly.

From then on, an anger habit operates automatically when the event which stimulates/triggers it occurs. The anger reaction has become programmed in your unconscious. It is then part of your emotional and behavioral memory.

As you can see, we form anger habits involving the automatic activation of angry thoughts, beliefs, emotions, and behaviors which are instantly triggered by the offending event or situation. And we have an unlimited capacity to form anger habits, such that they can come to be the dominant force in one's life. This is the bad news.

The good news is that you can change your anger habits and eliminate your anger reactions as soon as you are ready to make the necessary changes. The vital information in this book is all about helping you to do just that.

Chapter 3

Brian's Anger Issues

Violation of Trust, Disrespect, Offense, and Tricked or Deceived

The following stories are my personal experiences. And although I am not proud of getting angry and wasting my time, thoughts, and emotions on anger issues, I am sharing some of my experiences with you so that you can understand the costs involved with anger and how to avoid similar mistakes. The Core Emotional Issues (Chapter 1) described in my experiences that follow, are programmed or automated anger habits that I developed in myself early in my life, without realizing what I was developing.

The Prom: Relationship Abuse

When I was in high school in Orlando, Florida, I had been steadily dating a young lady from a different school who I considered to be my girlfriend. After two years, she broke up with me at the beginning of my senior year. I was clueless as to why she had broken up with me, and so typically, I felt very angry about it. Nevertheless, I started forming some new friendships and moving on with my high school social life.

Then one day, near the end of the school year, I got a call from my former girlfriend. She was very sweet, and she wanted to get back together in our relationship. I was delighted. At that time in my life, I was slow to form close relationships, and so I had been fairly lonely since my girlfriend had broken up with me. A few weeks after we started dating again, my girlfriend asked me who I was going to take to the Senior Prom. I told her that I had not asked anyone yet, and then I asked her if she would go with me to both of our proms.

When the day of the Senior Proms arrived, I was very excited. However by the end of the night, I felt that my girlfriend had been neglecting me in favor of her friends at her Prom. I was not having a good time. Warning signals should have been going off in my brain, but I was not mature enough to comprehend the reality of the situation.

The typical after-prom event at my school was to go out for a late meal after the prom and then to go to Daytona Beach, Florida the next day. As I was still clueless about my girlfriend's real feelings about me, I asked her where she wanted to go to eat and what time she wanted me to pick her up the next day. She replied that she wanted to go home

Chapter 3: Brian's Anger Issues

without eating and that she did not want to go to the beach the next day because it would mess up her hairdo.

    At that point, I got very angry, because I suddenly realized that I had just spent a lot of money on a date with a girl who did not really want to be my girlfriend or spend any quality time with me. I realized that she had just been using me to get to go to her Prom when it seemed to her that she was not going to be invited to go by someone from her school. There was very little conversation between us as I drove her home. Fortunately for me I had been taught very well by my mother and by what I had observed in life to not be verbally or physically abusive to females. But the angry silence in the car was very thick.

    After I left her at her house, I spent a certain amount of extra tire rubber on her driveway as I started to drive my car home that night ("that will teach her to not abuse me"), and then I wasted a lot of mental and emotional energy over the next several months being angry at being used by a young woman I had loved and trusted. Tricked, deceived, violation of trust—Grrrrr!

    My ***immature and false belief and so false expectations*** about my former girlfriend was that her attitude or morality about dating was the same as mine. If our roles were reversed, I would never have made up with a girl just so that she could spend a lot of money to take me to the prom and then immediately break up with her again.
    My false belief was exploded by my prom experience, and that really hurt. I was deeply offended.

The Gas Station: Coworker Abuse

After my junior year in high school, I got a summer job as a gas station attendant back when people pumped your gas, checked your oil, and washed your car windows without being asked or paid extra to do so. My coworker was a man in his 40s who was probably at the height of his employment opportunities. Even though we were quite different I got along with him pretty well, because I liked all sorts of people, even at that immature age.

Everything was fine between us for 2 months as we worked together at the gas station. I suppose that I grew to trust him and feel safe to work effectively with him. And then suddenly, a real shocker came my way when my coworker lied to our boss claiming that I had done something wrong when in fact the fault was his. I was furious, and I angrily threatened my coworker saying that I would make him very sorry if he ever did that again. Violation of trust—Grrrrr!

Lying is **Taker** Behavior (Chapter 4). My anger resulted not from his negative behavioral choice, but rather from my ***false beliefs and expectations*** of him. I got angry because I had mistakenly assumed that since I would never have lied and blamed him for my mistakes, surely my coworker would treat me the same way. My mistaken trust in my coworker was violated. Had I accurately known his moral values, I would have been more careful, and perhaps I would have made other choices like speaking to our boss about the issue or defending my honesty. I may even have

Chapter 3: Brian's Anger Issues

decided to find work elsewhere. But I didn't have the maturity to understand my coworker's true nature at that time in my life.

Valet Services: Customer Abuse

Once, when I was in my later 20s, I owned and operated a valet parking service at a four star restaurant in Tampa, Florida. As is true of valet parking services everywhere, my service had reserved parking spaces where we parked our customers' cars each night. It often happened that a restaurant customer either did not know that our spaces were reserved or chose to ignore the reserved sign. In either case, my policy was to kindly inform or have one of my employees inform the customer that the space was a valet parking space and to direct the customer to the nearby general parking lot.

This policy was very effective for several years, because the restaurant customers always moved their cars when we asked them to while providing an alternate parking solution for them that was reasonable. Then one night, a customer not only refused to move his car when I asked him to, but he was also arrogant and rude about his refusal.

Needless to say, I did not like the refusal, the arrogance, or the rudeness. I was not mature enough to just ignore the customer's bad behavior or feel sorry for his ignorance. Instead I got angry, and then I got even. Because a dinner meal at the restaurant took about 2-3 hours, I waited nearly two hours and then I parked one car two inches from the left side of the arrogant customer's car and another car two inches from the right side of the arrogant customer's car. Then I waited for him to come out of the restaurant.

When he finally did, he quickly realized that he could not get into his car. He got immediately angry, because I suppose that he realized that I did the parking on both sides of his car on purpose. He quickly approached me and demanded that I immediately move the cars by his. I honestly told him that we were busy just then and that I would get to it in a bit. The "getting even" felt good. From my perspective, justice had been properly served.

If you have ever been treated rudely by someone who was arrogant, you may be feeling quite satisfied just now by this rude man getting just what he deserved. However you may lose that feeling when you read about what my anger-motivated "getting even" cost me. I had not yet learned that when someone like this arrogant customer gets into a dispute or conflict with someone like me (with my positive moral standards), the arrogant person always wins in the near term (but not in the long term).

A **Taker** (Chapter 4) like this man was at that time is more willing to do negative or unjust things to win the dispute or conflict than a **Balancer** (Chapter 4) like I was at that time, who has higher moral standards.

After I told the arrogant customer that I could not move the surrounding cars right away, he immediately went to find the restaurant owner. After about ten minutes, the

Chapter 3: Brian's Anger Issues 23

restaurant owner summoned me to his office. When I arrived, I found the owner with the arrogant customer. The owner told me that I was to apologize to the customer and pay for a dinner-for-two gift certificate for the customer as a tangible apology in addition to my verbal one.

As you can imagine, that dish of "humble pie" was difficult for me to "eat", but I did what the restaurant owner required of me. I painfully learned that my angry motivated "getting even" cost was much more expensive than the "getting even" benefit of seeing justice served after being offended by an arrogant man. Devaluation, disrespect, and then financial abuse—Grrr!

My first *false belief* about this situation, was that I could politely ask anyone to respect my business interests, and they would simply comply. My second *false belief* was that I could use nonviolent revenge to teach a lesson to an arrogant person with little or no reprisal from him. My third *false belief* was that I and my business were more important to the restaurateur than his customer and his business interests.

More Humble Pie and Anger

During my college years at the University of South Florida and for five additional years after I had graduated, I worked first as a waiter and then, as previously mentioned, the owner and operator of the valet parking service for a four star restaurant in Tampa, Florida. I really liked and respected the owner.

Chapter 3: Brian's Anger Issues

Later in my life, I realized that the restaurant owner had built and maintained a great restaurant organization, in terms of consistently providing the highest quality of food and services in his restaurant. And, I greatly valued the experience and knowledge that I had gained while working there for ten years, about how to build and lead a very high quality organization/business.

At the end of 1979, I gave up the valet parking service to attend graduate school at the University of Georgia. As it so happened after graduate school, my first teaching appointment was back in Lakeland, Florida at Florida Southern College. I was teaching a business psychology course there, and I thought that it would be a great idea to take my class to the restaurant in Tampa where I used to work, to show them what a high quality organization was like from the inside, perhaps also having the opportunity to get some words of wisdom from the owner.

When we arrived at the restaurant, the owner kindly consented to give my class a tour of his restaurant so that they could see the quality of his organization. However at the end of the tour, my former boss, the owner, turned to me and confronted me in front of my students about the incident with the arrogant customer and some of the other immaturities of my young adulthood.

The restaurant owner did this apparently to embarrass and belittle me, perhaps because he was envious that I had greatly improved my professional life or because he never

Chapter 3: Brian's Anger Issues

really liked or respected me very much. Although I hid it, I got very angry for this major violation of trust and respect. Violation of Trust and Disrespect—Grrr!

While his treatment of me was very inappropriate, the reason that I got mad was I had a *false expectation* that my former boss was trustworthy and that he respected me for the years of service that I had given him. Boy was I mistaken about that!

Over the many years of my life, in addition to the few true stories that I have shared with you, I have been angry with my spouse, my children, my parents, my siblings, my friends, my associates, my coworkers, my employees, my bosses, rude and dangerous drivers, and a lots of others. The trouble is that never has getting angry with any of them ever turned out well for me or for them in the long run.

Anger is a mistake. I have wasted a great deal of my life feeling it and cleaning up the messes that I made inside myself and in various relationships, while being angry. Anger saps your mental and emotional energy that could be spent on positive and productive matters, it costs you precious time, and it deprives you of the happiness that could otherwise be yours!

One reason that we get angry with others is because we do not accurately understand their fundamental moral nature or maturity very well. The next chapter about Takers, Balancers, and Givers will hopefully give you a better understanding of this problem.

Chapter 4

Takers, Balancers & Givers

Moral Development Levels: Why People Do and Do Not Unconsciously Stimulate or Trigger Anger in Others

    This chapter will help you better understand true human nature, and consequently, what to expect from anyone, from distant strangers and people that you only meet and briefly associate with to your work associates, friends, family, and loved ones. The better you understand what a person can or cannot do, think, or feel, the more realistic your expectations of them will be. As a result, you will have a greater understanding of their true capacities and less or no anger towards them when they do seemingly or real unfair or offensive things concerning you or others.

Chapter 4: Takers, Balancers, & Givers

The vital piece of understanding, which incorporates what you learn in this and other chapters, and which is My Most Important Anger Elimination Insight, will be explained in Chapter 20.

After many years of studying and observing people, I have developed a simple classification system which divides all of humanity into three general categories of moral development as it relates to fairness/justice and the ideal positive treatment of others. The categories are Takers, Balancers, and Givers.

When considering morality in this chapter, I include behavior and the absence of behavior, thoughts and beliefs and the absence of them, as well as emotions and the absences of them. This means that there are things that we do (behaviors) that are good and bad, and there are things that we do not do (behaviors) that by not doing are good or bad. The same concepts of doing and not doing, applies to thoughts, beliefs, and emotions as well.

Please realize that none of us are 100% defined by one of the major Taker, Balancer, or Giver moral categories. Although each of us is generally best represented by only one of these categories, most of us have different aspects of our selves and lives represented by two or three of these categories depending on our personality, past life experiences, current life situations, and maturity. Hence, almost all of us take, balance, and/or give in different situations and with different people.

Chapter 4: Takers, Balancers, & Givers

Takers

First of all, let me describe Takers, who mostly treat and think about others in a negative way. In terms of civilized behavior, maturity, good thoughts, etc., Takers are at the lowest level. In general, they are selfish and ignorant. Selfish, because most of what they do or do not do, think or do not think, believe or do not believe, and feel or do not feel has to do with what they think is good for them without much interest or concern about how it affects others. What they want or need, they take from others. This taking includes, but is not limited to such things as material possessions, safety, time, money, pleasure, friendships, happiness, opportunities, jobs, ideas, and credit for accomplishments.

Takers are also generally ignorant, because they really do not understand that their taking behaviors and attitudes are harming themselves as well as others. They are unskilled in or ignorant about better ways of behaving, thinking, believing, and feeling. Examples of Takers include, but are not limited to liars, selfish people, adulterers, gossips, persecutors, thieves, murderers, pimps, con artists, embezzlers, tyrants, greedy individuals, vandals, destroyers, unethical business men and women, manipulators, narcissists, physical/verbal/sexual/emotional abusers, rapists, pedophiles, bullies, employees who cheat their employers out of a reasonable amount and quality of work, employers who mistreat or otherwise cheat their employees by not paying them a fair wage for work done, and leaders who seek to take away the freedoms of the people that they lead.

Chapter 4: Takers, Balancers, & Givers

Takers are the greatest source of the injustices, offenses, harm, damage, and unfairness inflicted upon each other and upon the rest of the population with whom they associate. Nevertheless, as I mentioned previously, most Takers may also act as Balancers or even Givers at times, although it is usually only infrequently. Takers may balance (act fairly) or even give (act generously and kindly) with certain people and in certain situations. However, most of the time, they take: the worst of the Takers doing 100% taking, and the best of the Takers doing 51% taking with the remainder of their behavior being mostly balancing and a little giving.

As you may already realize, Takers cause the most violations of others' Core Emotional Issues (Chapter 2) resulting in the stimulation/triggering of a lot of anger.

I have observed that Takers represent about 16% of the population in most of the cultures and countries around the world and are much more abundant in a few of the worst of the world's cultures and countries. Something else that it is also important to know, is that the harsher the conditions in a culture or a country, the greater the percentage of Takers and the fewer Givers and Balancers. By harsh, I do not mean low technology, low resources, undeveloped high culture, or poverty necessarily. I mean that the people in the culture treat each other harshly such as in ghetto conditions, long civil or other wars, strong prejudice and discrimination conditions, low personal freedoms, tyrannical government, etc.

Balancers

Balancers, treat and think about others fairly, as best that they understand this, and represent about 68% of the population of most cultures and countries. Those in this category who are the least morally developed, do a lot of taking, but no more than 49% of what they do is taking, and those who are more morally developed do a fair amount of giving in addition to their balancing. Subsequently, the more morally developed Balancers do very little taking and a reasonable amount of giving, but not as much giving (treating and thinking about others generously and kindly) as balancing (treating and thinking about others fairly).

By Balancer, I mean that these individuals are careful to try to follow the rules of justice or fairness. Meaning they keep track of what is done to or for them and what they do for or to others. Balancers generally and most often believe in and are committed to fairness or justice. What you do for them, they feel obligated to do for you. What they do for you, they expect you to reciprocate. In most respects, this is really not a bad way to live.

Balancers' friendships, marriages, and other relationships or associations involve judging the value of, and keeping track of the number of contributions to the relationship by the other person involved in the relationship. They tend to get angry about people who they believe do not contribute their fair share of whatever to the relationship.

And, very importantly, a Balancer's anger often results from their wrong perceptions involving the overvaluing of their personal contributions to a relationship or situation and undervaluing the other person's contributions.

Subsequently, a 50/50 balanced relationship is ultimately doomed to failure. Balancers are the good and honorable people of the world. Justice and fairness is their standard and goal.

Balancers generally do not forgive until the offending party apologizes, makes "payment" for the offense, or receives a deserved bad consequence. In many cases, they never totally forgive those who have offended them, because that they believe that justice or fairness has not been sufficiently restored.

Givers

Givers represent about 16% of the world population and are those individuals who, in various good ways think about and act on behalf of others because it is the right thing to do. None of them are perfect, although they may seem to be so, because they do little to no taking.

Givers are not particularly interested in, nor do they care about getting something in return for what they do for others (balancing). They are the most morally developed group of the three general types of people that I am describing in this chapter.

Givers are people who "clean up the messes" that other people make in their own lives and in their relationships, and the "messes" that others make in the physical environment. They typically are doing all kinds of good deeds quietly. They are consistently and diligently making the world a better place for all of us physically, educationally, emotionally, socially, cognitively, and spiritually, etc.

The vast majority of givers will never be publicly know or appreciated, since they do what they do for the sake of doing the right thing, not for the rewards of fame and fortune. The Givers who are the most mature quietly bring many positive changes to our world cultures.

Some of those Givers who are more widely known are people like Shakyamuni Buddha, William Tyndale, Mother Theresa, Albert Switzer, Billy Graham, Julie B. Beck, Martin Luther King, Clara Barton, Mahatma Gandhi, Rosemary M. Wixom, Gordon B. Hinckley, Elaine S. Dalton, Thomas S. Monson, Florence Nightingale, Louis Pasteur, Abraham Lincoln, Dalai Lama, and Nelson Mandela.

Whenever I learn about, meet, or interact with someone from this moral category, my life is always much better for it.

Givers do not create injustice or unfairness in general, or much at all. But, what they do or do not do can be perceived by others, who are less mature and wise, as unfair or unjust even though no unfairness or injustice has actually occurred. Of course, some of Givers' thinking, beliefs, actions, and emotions are balancing instead of giving in nature, and some of them may even do a little selfish taking at times.

Takers very often and some Balancers sometimes get angry at Givers because they envy Givers for who they are, or even because seeing or being around Givers results in them feeling badly about their own selfishness and ignorance. Takers tend to think that Givers are fools or suckers, and that they deserve to be taken advantage of. And unfortunately, Takers often do try to or succeed at taking advantage of or otherwise harming Givers.

Traditional marriages that reach their full potential for happiness and longevity involve a man and a woman who initially are or have both matured to be Givers. The best parents are also Givers, because they strive to only do for their children what is right and best. They give their children rules, discipline, responsibility, accountability, love, guidance, support, encouragement, and the finest example of a mature and happy person.

The best and most respected members of any family, organization, or culture are Givers. The best leaders, workers, and teachers are Givers. And, Givers are the best friends.

Chapter 5

Justice: "Balancing The Scales"

The Relationship of Anger to the Violation of Justice or Fairness

Most of us, but especially males, place a high emotional value on justice and fairness. While there is not anything inherently wrong with this, it can become a major generator of anger and other related problems when high emotional value is combined with wrong or inaccurate thoughts and beliefs about justice.

In the previous chapter I presented three general categories or levels of human moral development. As you recall, the people who are represented by these levels are referred to as Takers, Balancers, and Givers. Each of these types of individuals is interested in justice, but each type thinks about and deals with justice in a different way.

Chapter 5: Justice: "Balancing The Scales"

Takers are highly focused on justice or what they perceive to be fairness---for themselves, but not for others.

When Takers are hindered or harmed, or believe that they have been hindered or harmed, they believe that they need swift justice to be administered to the other. This is often done overtly or covertly by the Taker personally, to anyone who wrongs them or who they think has wronged them.

Takers believe that they deserve mercy, or a "pass" if it so happens that they get caught for wronging others. And often they do not even care that they harm or wrong others.

Balancers are also highly focused on justice and believe it should be administered universally---to both themselves and others. They need and seek to achieve balanced "Scales of Justice" in almost all matters.

Balancers are much less likely than Takers to seek revenge or try to administer punishments to others themselves. Their problem, as mentioned previously, is that they typically consciously or unconsciously overestimate the value of their positive contributions to relationship or situation and underestimate the value of their negative contributions. And, in relation to the other or others involved, the Balancer typically consciously or unconsciously underestimates the value of the other or others positive contributions to relationship or situation and overestimates the value of their negative contributions.

Givers are much less interested in justice/fairness and are much more interested in mercy. But they seek or administer justice when they think it will be developmentally better for the offender than mercy. In those cases justice is actually mercy.

What Givers know, is that even though many things seem or are unfair and unjust in the short-term, everything is just and fair in the long-term. Most people do not understand this reality, either because they have not lived long enough or have not paid enough attention to observe this for the fact that it is. In some cases, the long-term takes years, decades, centuries, or even millennia for justice to become balanced when it is has been unbalanced.

With the truth that justice takes care of itself in mind, and when we really accept it as the truth, there is little or no need for individuals to focus on seeking to personally administer justice to those who offend them. This is because justice always happens in the long-term.

When a person realizes and accepts this fact about justice mentally and emotionally, or even increases in their capacity to realize and accept it, then getting angry because of injustice and unfairness loses its meaning and potency. As a result, anger is reduced.

That being said, it is still correct for parents to do the appropriate things to administer just corrections or discipline to those family members who cause harm to their family members or non-family members, for business or

Chapter 5: Justice: "Balancing The Scales"

organizational leaders to do the appropriate things to administer just corrections or discipline to those business or organizational members who need it, and for governments to do the appropriate things to administer just corrections or discipline to those citizens in the culture who need that.

These justice restoring corrections are acceptable, and in most cases necessary, because families, businesses, organizations, and governments have a responsibility to protect their members' or citizens' rights and well being, and a responsibility to help their offending or justice-violating members or citizens change their wrong/offending behaviors to non-offending, non-justice violating behaviors.

Although many individuals do not understand or accept the reality of long term justice, the cultures of the world, in some ways, recognize the reality of long-term justice and fairness. Some world cultures express an understanding of long term justice in the following colloquial terms: "What goes around comes around", "The Law of the Harvest" or "What you sow, you reap", "Quid pro quo", "Tit for tat", "Un bon chat, bon rat", and "Karma".

The bottom line, is that abuse of others in any form (violation of justice) actually guarantees that you will get to experience the same sort, or similar sort, of violation of justice personally, or observe it happening to others that you care about. The positive objective of this relationship, is that you will learn to do your best to eliminate injustice towards others that results from what you think, believe, feel, and do, or what you fail to think, believe, feel, or do.

Chapter 6

The Great & Dreadful Anger Path

How You Might "Experiment" as You Work to Change Your Anger Habits

In 1993, I was experiencing a very interesting opportunity to educate and consult with a few individuals who were deeply concerned about overcoming very difficult barriers that they were then facing in their lives. One of those individuals needed to better understand his anger and to learn to control it, thus reducing the personal and relationship problems which came from his frequent bouts of anger. To honor his privacy, I will call him Sam.

Sam wanted to know how to reduce his strong anger reactions to various situations and people so that he would have less problems and more happiness. At that time in my life, I had not thought very carefully about how we develop

Chapter 6: The Great & Dreadful Anger Path

anger or how it is a programmed habit that we can change once we learn the correct way to do that. I also had not thought specifically about how to teach someone else to reduce their anger.

Consequently, when Sam asked me to explain how he could reduce his anger, I began to give anger some serious consideration and research. My desire was to give him and others the best developmental information possible and the highest chance for successful change.

What I learned, and what I now teach is:

First, angers are thoughts/beliefs/emotions/behaviors (TBEB) habits which we develop early in our lives in relation to certain things that we experience or are deprived of.

Second, there is an easily understandable internal (thoughts, beliefs, emotions) path that we experience when we develop an anger habit.

And **Third**, we can change an anger habit (which we have unconsciously programmed) by choosing to "go down" the same internal path in a different, positive, healthier way.

Thought/Belief/Emotion/Behavior (TBEB) habits are habits that we form by the choices that we make in life, whether we are conscious of the choice or not (and most of the time we are not consciously aware of our choices). If we choose to think or not think certain things when we see someone or experience some specific thing, those thoughts and related thoughts or that absence of thoughts of certain types, are automatically programmed in our memory and are brought to our conscious or near-conscious mind automatically whenever the person or experience, or even similar or related people or experiences happen in our lives. This same process of automating or programming applies to beliefs, emotions, and our behaviors.

A habit is just a shortcut in our mind/memory that reflects what we have chosen in the past in relation to what happened or failed to happen and/or who was involved. We have an unlimited capacity to create and maintain these habit shortcuts. That is quite useful, because we have a very limited capacity in our conscious attention. As I have mentioned before, just try to keep in your conscious thoughts all of the things (like the position of every part of your body, where you are looking, the exact series of contractions and relaxations of the many muscles that are involve in balancing your body correctly and causing the correct parts to move you forward in the correct way, etc.) that are vital to being able to walk one step and you will see what I mean.

You will see that I use the concept of "Negative External Thoughts" in the following diagram of The Anger Path. I will not explain that concept fully here, but to be brief, "Negative External Thoughts" is one of the four sources of human thought. I will discuss more about The Four Sources of Thoughts in Chapter 13.

Chapter 6: The Great & Dreadful Anger Path   41

The Anger Path

Some event occurs (Chapter 2, Step 1-definition of "event").

You become or are consciously aware of the event.
Negative External Thoughts may encourage you to notice the event.

You choose to believe, or have previously chosen to believe that the event is emotionally important to you.
This belief may be the result of Negative External Thoughts and/or your own previous experiences.

You choose to believe that this event is unjust/unfair/unnecessary and that it harms or will harm you or some cared-about other person in some way.
Negative External Thoughts encourage this belief.

You automatically experience emotional pain as a natural consequence of your chosen belief.

You have a strong (most often unconscious) desire to eliminate your emotional pain as soon as possible.
Negative External Thoughts encourage this desire.

⇩

You unconsciously choose to convert the emotional arousal of pain into the emotion of anger by mentally relabeling the physiological emotional arousal as anger.
Negative External Thoughts encourage this conversion

⇩

You are motivated and energized to mentally, verbally, and/or behaviorally choose to seek revenge and/or the restoration of justice and fairness.
Negative External Thoughts encourage this choice

This attempted restoration of justice and fairness can be limited to only thoughts, emotions, and beliefs or can expand to actions or absence of actions which you believe will achieve restoration of justice or revenge.

By continually repeating the preceding anger path process, or even by having only one very emotionally meaningful experience like this, the process becomes automated and shortened (an anger habit is created).

The functional effect of this in your life is that the same disturbing or offending event or one similar to it, will now automatically stimulate/trigger/activate your immediate response of anger and its associated thoughts, beliefs,

Chapter 6: The Great & Dreadful Anger Path

and behaviors, without your conscious awareness. That is a programmed anger habit

Once I personally understood how this process worked, I decided to try changing my anger habits by remaining consciously aware of my anger and what I was thinking and believing unconsciously to create or trigger the anger. I was convinced that if I reversed the process a bit at a time, I could get rid of my anger habits.

At first this meant that I would have to choose emotional pain instead of anger when I was harmed or offended or had the potential to be harmed or offended. Better still, to eliminate the emotional reaction altogether, I would have to change the way I thought about people, things, situations, and events which in some way might usually harm or offend me or others that I cared about.

My first test of my theory about this systematic anger reduction process occurred at my home. I had a general *false belief* that in any disagreement with someone else, I would be the one that would always be right.

Many years ago, my wife and I, being spousal "works in progress", got into an emotional argument about something that now I cannot even remember. I had previously decided that I wanted to remain consciously aware of being angry before it ramped up to maximum anger. Because becoming or remaining consciously aware of our thoughts, beliefs, emotions, and/or behaviors, allows us to choose different ones, and so form different automated habits. And so in the middle of our war of words, I started to pay conscious attention to my anger, instead of how "unreasonable", "hurtful", and "wrong" I thought/believed that my wife was being.

At that point, I stopped arguing, muttered some reason for leaving, walked out of the room, and went to sit in our car in the garage. I did not do that to make my wife mad as I had done in the past by walking away to frustrate her attempts to communicate or "win" the argument.

While sitting in the car, I decided to let, the key word here being 'let', myself feel hurt instead of angry over the "offenses" that had occurred to start the argument and those "offenses" which had been added on during the heat of our brief angry exchange.

I thought it would be easy to let myself feel emotionally hurt rather than angry. It was not! I found to my surprise that I really had to struggle again and again to let the emotional pain come, because I wanted to feel angry and felt I deserved to feel that way.

Finally after about 30 minutes of internal struggling with these emotions, I allowed myself to just feel emotionally hurt. That hurt a lot in my emotions, and as I felt this painful emotion, I wept about the things that had led to the argument, the things that had been said in the argument, and what all of those things represented in terms of harm to us and our marital relationship.

Chapter 6: The Great & Dreadful Anger Path

Needless to say, this was not a fun experience. It was painful and humbling. However, I also learned that once I let it happen, the emotional pain did not take as long to subside and disappear as I had thought or feared that it might.

At that point, when the emotional pain had naturally diminished, I went back into the house, found my wife, and reconciled our differences without anger. I was amazed to learn that in comparison to previous anger experiences of the same type and magnitude, this experience was resolved in a tenth of the time and with a tenth of the mental and emotional cost.

In other words, the part of the mess that I had made in our relationship was a lot easier and a lot less costly to "clean up" because of eliminating my anger in favor of accepting the emotional pain (whether from the point of view of a Balancer, I deserved the pain or not).

From that point in my life on, I practiced what I had learned, just as I described, and I got better and better at reducing my anger. As I mentioned before, I knew that there was probably more that I could do to reduce and even eliminate my anger. But I was glad indeed that I was gaining understanding and making progress in my maturity and happiness.

I certainly believe that it is better to also eliminate the emotional pain reaction altogether when one is offended or wronged in some way. At the time described, I realized and believed that I could also learn to change the way that I thought and believed about things which in some way would usually harm or offend me or potentially could harm or offend me.

As I got better at staying consciously aware of what offended me, why it did offend me, and consciously aware of my thoughts and beliefs about the offending or harming event, I began to have some success at not even allowing my emotions to get hurt in the first place.

I thus avoided contention, emotional pain, the ineffective behavior of distancing myself from someone for emotional "protection", and, of course, creating some sort of relationship mess to clean up.

At that point in time, I figured that what I was doing was the best that I could do to reduce my anger about things that did not go the way that I wanted. I believed that anger elimination was a very distant goal that I might not even achieve over the rest of my life. But, as is often true, I was in for a major surprise that I will discuss in Chapter 20, "My Most Important Insight About Anger Elimination".

In the next chapter, I continue with some simple guidance to help you better understand about anger habits and how to change them.

Chapter 7

Reducing Anger By Replacing Anger Habits

How to Significantly Reduce or Eliminate Your Anger Habits

You may already realize or know that there are things that cause you to automatically feel the emotions of sad, lonely, disgusted, happy, angry, surprised, discouraged, depressed, afraid, excited, and so forth. But do you know how those emotional reactions got programmed in your unconscious in the first place? And, of greater importance, do you know how to change your emotional habits that you want to change? Well, that is what this chapter is all about, as it builds on what was presented in Chapter 6.

Each of us is born with the ability to generate any one of the hundreds of possible human emotions. The following list of emotions, is only a small sampling emotions, and there are many more which are various combinations of these.

Chapter 7: Replacing Your Anger Habits

Because the focus of this Chapter is about any level of anger, I have highlighted the emotional variations below that are most related to anger.

Able, Adequate, Adoration, Affection, **Agitation**, Agonized, **Aggravation**, Alarmed, Alienation, Altruistic, Amazed, Amused, **Angry**, Anguish, **Annoyed**, Anxious, Apprehensive, Aroused, Astonishment, Attraction, Belonging, Betrayed, Bewildered, **Bitter**, Bliss, Bold, Bonded, Bored, Brave, Burdened, Calm, Capable, Caring, Cautious, Charmed, Cheerful, Comfortable, Competitive, Concerned, Confident, Conflicted, Confused, Connected, Contempt, Contentment, Delight, Depressed, Desire, Despair, Destructive, Determined, Devalued, Disadvantaged, Disappointed, Disgusted, Dismay, Displeasure, Distracted, Distress, Doubtful, Downcast, Dread, Dumbfounded, Eager, Ecstasy, Elation, Embarrassed, Empathetic, Energetic, Enjoyment, **Enraged**, Enthrallment, Enthused, Euphoria, **Exasperated**, Excited, Exhausted, Exhilarated, Expectant, Fascinated, Fear, Fondness, Forgiving, Free, Friendly, Fright, Frisky, **Frustrated**, **Fury**, Gaiety, Glad, Gloom, Good, Great, **Grouchy**, Guilty, Happy, Harassed, **Hate**, Helpful, Hesitant, Homesick, Hopeful, Horror, **Hostile**, Humble, Humiliated, Hurt, Hysteria, Ignored, Impatient, Indifferent, Infatuation, Insecurity, Inspired, Intimidated, **Irritated**, Isolated, Jealous, Joy, Jubilation, Jumpy, **Loathing**, Longing, Lost, Love, Lust, **Mad**, Manipulated, Melancholy, Miserable, Mortification, Neglect, Nervousness, Obnoxious, Obsession, Optimism, Overwhelmed, Panic, Passion, Peaceful, Philanthropic, Pity, Platonic, Pleasant, Pleasure, Positive, Powerful, Pressured, Proud, Regret,

Chapter 7: Replacing Your Anger Habits

Relaxed, Relieved, Religious, Remorse, **Resentment**, Revulsion, Romantic, Sad, Safe, Satisfied, Scared, Sentimental, Shame, Shocked, Suffering, Surprised, Suspicious, Sympathetic, Tenseness, Terror, Thrill, Tired, Torment, Uncomfortable, Uneasy, **Unforgiving**, Unhappy, Unity, **Used**, Wary, Wasteful, Weary, Wellbeing, Withdrawn, Worried, **Wrath**, and Zest.

We are born with the ability to form habits, or to have our thoughts, beliefs, emotions, and behaviors become automated or programmed. Fortunately, we have the ability to consciously choose what we think, believe, feel, and do. It is our choices about the things we think, believe, feel, and do, that cause them to become automated responses or habits. And so, it is also our conscious choices about the things we think, believe, feel, and do that allows us to change our automated programming.

After we are born, we have a continuing stream of greatly varying life experiences that we record in our unconscious programming/memory and thus connect in very complex ways, but through a relatively simple to understand process, to our thoughts, beliefs, emotions, and behaviors.

Sometimes, only one strong or meaningful experience is enough to form a strong automated habit. For instance, when as a baby I was bitten in the face by a dog, I immediately programmed a fear reaction to that dog, and quickly formed/generalized an automatic fear reaction to all other dogs. That is a dog phobia. Although my original fear was associated with only one specific dog, my phobic fear reaction was always activated/triggered by seeing any dog, hearing any dog bark, thinking about any dog, or almost anything else relating to dogs.

By my fear being activated or triggered, I mean that I automatically felt the emotion of fear and the usual physical reactions to it, without having to decide to feel fear. I also had my thoughts filled with thoughts of how to avoid, protect myself from, or get away from the dog. I automatically believed that I was in danger, which I almost never really was, and I almost always acted out the behaviors of avoidance or escape.

With experience, all of our emotions get automated or programmed to just immediately turn on when certain things happen or do not happen, when we think about or interact with certain people, and when certain conditions do or don't exist.

So, when something happens or does not happen in relation to our specific core emotional issues, we do not have to think about why we should be angry or how to think angry thoughts, we just feel angry, think the angry thoughts, and often do some angry behaviors. These reactions were programmed, habituated, or automated by our previous conscious or unconscious choice or choices about a similar situation, stimuli, or person, like the one that we are currently experiencing, which triggers our anger.

Just like what was illustrated in the Anger Path that I described in Chapter 6, all habits, or automatic emotional

Chapter 7: Replacing Your Anger Habits

reactions in this case, are formed in the same way that I have diagramed next. They become a part of our "programming" or what various psychologists call our memory, or unconscious.

I am repeating this programming process with greater detail in this chapter, so that it is more understandable, and more helpful, as you work to replace your anger habits.

Our "programming" is a good thing when we have programmed something that is good for our life. But it becomes problematic when we unknowingly have programmed something like anger responses to lots of different situations related to our Core Emotional Issues. Or it is a problem when we unknowingly program ourselves to things that we have chosen/learned to fear.

Steps to Forming a Habit

First, some *Event* occurs (Chapter 2, Step 1-definition of "event").

Second, you are *Aware* of the *Event*, meaning that you are consciously paying attention to it. Lots of things (events) are happening near us all of the time, but we are only consciously aware of a very few of them at a any given time.

Third, you either already *Have a Belief* or you *Form a Belief* that the *Event* is *Emotionally Important* to you. Positive and Negative External sources most often encourage this *Belief* formation. The source doing the encouraging depends on whether the belief will be beneficial for you or harmful for you.

⇩

Fourth, you *Choose to Believe* that the *Event* harms (or will harm) or benefits (or will benefit) you or someone that you care about in some way. External sources most often encourage this *Choice*.

⇩

Fifth, if you *Believe* that the *Event* harms you or someone that you care about in some way, you *Automatically React* with Emotional Pain, Emotional Anger, or Emotional Fear, depending on which one is a natural consequence of your Belief, or that has been previously programmed in your unconscious. In addition you automatically activate *Thoughts, Body/Physiological Responses, and Behaviors* related to the emotion that fits the *Belief*.

Or...

If you *Believe* that the *Event* helps or benefits you or someone that you care about in some way, you *Automatically React* with Emotional Happiness, Joy, Satisfaction, Peace, or Calmness, depending on which one is a natural consequence of your belief or has been previously

Chapter 7: Replacing Your Anger Habits

programmed in your unconscious/memory. In addition you automatically activate *Thoughts, Physiological Responses, and Behaviors* related to the emotion that fits the *Belief.*

Sixth, every time the *Event* is experienced and the above process is *Repeated,* it *Strengthens and Quickens* the emotional reaction/reactions, unless you choose to do something different than what you have done in the past about your *Thoughts and Beliefs.*

Remember that the vast amount of what we think, believe, feel, and do has been automated or has become a habit. We mostly react to things in our lives unconsciously, or on auto pilot, all of the time that we are awake. And we very likely do the same in our dreams as well. Again, this is what I refer to as our programming.

Fortunately, you can change any of your habits or your programming. It requires staying consciously aware of what you are thinking and feeling when the habit is being stimulated by some event, situation, or person. For instance, an event occurs. You feel angry. You are consciously aware of your building anger. You choose to think and believe differently about the situation, even the exact opposite of the thoughts or beliefs that are associated with your anger.

Consequently, your feelings of anger shrink or disappear. As you learn to consciously stay aware of thoughts and emotions that you want to change, and you repeat your thought and belief replacements again and again, you will cease to be automatically angry in that particular situation, about that event, or about that person's behavior.

How to Change Your Anger Habits/Programming

Before an anger stimulating event is taking place for you, do the following things:

1. Identify your Core Emotional Issues (Chapter 1). These are the ones of the 20 which are most important to you.

2. Make a true/honest commitment to change your anger habits to something more positive.

3. Identify specific positive opposite thoughts/beliefs for the negative thoughts/beliefs that are part of your anger path habit. It often helps to make and keep with you, 3x5 cards that each list a specific anger thought/belief, and its positive opposite thought/belief.

4. Practice becoming consciously aware of and staying consciously aware of your emotional reactions to specific events, situations, or persons, and their relationship to which of your thoughts and beliefs are associated with them.

Then, when some anger stimulating *Event* (or person's behavior, unfair situation, etc.) occurs,

Chapter 7: Replacing Your Anger Habits 55

strive to stay *Consciously Aware* of the *Event,* meaning you are consciously paying attention to it.

⇩

Pay focused conscious attention to the negative *Thoughts/Beliefs that you either already have*, or the negative *Thoughts/Beliefs that you are forming* about the event, the person's behavior or attitude, or the situation, and that are stimulating/causing you to feel angry.

⇩

Choose to consciously think the positive thoughts and beliefs that are the opposites of the anger stimulating thoughts and beliefs. You will feel awkward doing this at first, but you will get more and more skilled at this as the positive thoughts and beliefs become the new automatic responses. As you continue doing this, you will feel supported and encouraged by your progress.

⇩

When you *Believe* the positive beliefs and *Think* the positive thoughts about the *Event* (or person's behavior/attitude, unfair situation, etc.), in an automatic way, you will have replaced the old anger habit with something more positive. In addition you automatically activate *Thoughts, Physiological Responses, and Behaviors* related to the positive emotion that fit the new positive *Thoughts and Beliefs*.

Your new emotional responses will then be such things as Emotional Happiness, Joy, Satisfaction, Peace, and Calmness, depending on which ones are a natural consequence of your newly chosen positive beliefs.

⇩

Every time the *Event* (or person's behavior/attitude, unfair situation, etc.) is then experienced and the above process is *Repeated,* it *Strengthens and Quickens* your positive emotional reactions, unless you choose to do something different about your new positive *Thoughts and Beliefs.*

So, to summarize, all habits are formed from our choices, although we almost never realize that we are forming habits that are being continuously added to our personal internal programming and being modified by subsequent life experiences and choices.

All of your negative habits can be changed by your conscious choices. Your anger beliefs, thoughts, and behavioral habits can be replaced by their positive opposites through your conscious choices.

David's story is next. The experience described in that story may be like one of yours or like one of someone that you know very well. In any case, it is all about how to do **thorough forgiveness**, which of course naturally reduces anger.

Chapter 8

Reducing Anger: David's Story

True Forgiveness has 2 vital parts. Many of us do not want to forgive. And, few of us know how to thoroughly forgive.

One very important way to significantly reduce your anger is learning how to properly/completely and quickly forgive people who you believe have offended you or others that you care about, who you believe have unfairly dealt with you or others, or who you believe have wronged you or others in some way. In this chapter, I will discuss what real and total/complete forgiveness is, and how to achieve it.

A number of years ago, when my son, David, was around 8 years old, he taught me what **True Forgiveness** actually was. Up until that time, I believed, as do most us believe, that I understood how to forgive someone.

Chapter 8: Reducing Anger: David's Story

Boy was I wrong!

On this occasion of my **True Forgiveness** insight, my family and I were socially gathered in the master bedroom of our home, as we often were, each doing something personally interesting. I was sitting comfortably on my bed preparing my lectures for a psychology class, and my son David was trying to get my attention, because he wanted some quality father-son interaction.

What he wanted to do was "play wrestle" with me. I was willing to play wrestle with him, but because I was 6'2" and 230 pounds and he was 5' and 89 pounds, I knew that I would have to restrain myself in this playing a lot. I knew that by refraining from using my greater physical abilities, we would both have a good time play wrestling together. So, with that in mind, I agreed to play wrestle with David.

I laid my notes down on the far side of the bed, and we went at it with gusto. We both enjoyed it for several minutes until David suddenly felt emotionally overwhelmed and overpowered by our size and strength differences.

Then, while we were still wrestling, David reacted angrily by reaching over to the far side of the bed, grabbing my lecture notes, and ripping them in half. At first, I was very surprised and a bit angry. And then I immediately realized that the wrestling had gone on too long. David was not physically hurt, but he was emotionally hurt because of feeling powerless to "win".

Chapter 8: Reducing Anger: David's Story

Often as a child, I had experienced the same feelings as David did, when my childhood rough play went too far, leaving me hurt physically or emotionally. I was not very angry that David had destroyed my lecture notes (which were important to me), because I understood very personally what he was experiencing.

My reaction to this situation was that I immediately stopped our physical play, even though David wanted to continue. He asked me several times to start wrestling again, but each time I refused and told him that we had gone too far. I added that we were done for the day. Disappointed, he got up and left the room. And, I picked up my notepad and started working on my notes again while letting my mild anger dissipate.

After a few minutes, David came back to the side of my bed, stood beside me, and contritely told me that he was sorry for tearing up my notes. I told him that it was ok. And then I went back to my notes, feeling grateful that he had apologized and feeling free of the mild anger that I had previously felt toward David.

Then, David asked if we could wrestle again, and I said, no, that we had gone too far which had resulted in unhappiness and a loss of fun. I clearly remembered the bad feelings we had both experienced, and I did not want to risk creating them again for either of us.

At that point, I was feeling very wise and confident in my good parenting until David again stood by my bedside and said, "Dad, I said that I am sorry. Don't you forgive me?" His question hit me like a ton of bricks, because I suddenly realized that while I had done the first part of forgiveness, I had not done the second and probably the most important part.

I had let go of my brief angry feelings toward my son, and I thought that was what forgiveness was all about. However, what I had not done, was let my natural kind and happy feelings toward my son return to me. That is the second and final part of **True Forgiveness.**

So to repeat, **True Forgiveness** involves two basic parts. First, it involves choosing to let go of any and all negative emotions toward the person who we believe or who actually has done something wrong or has failed to do the right thing towards us or someone that we care about.

Any of us can do that when we really want to let go of our negative emotions, but we must give up any desires for revenge, retribution, or justice to be administered. Some people cannot even do this first necessary part of forgiveness, because they are not mature enough to do so. Consequently, they carry around a large conscious or unconscious, unhealed, emotional wound, sometimes for the rest of their lives.

Remember, forgiveness is Giver Behavior (Chapter 4), and is a gift that we give, almost always before someone "deserves" it, and because it is the right thing to do.

The second basic part of **True Forgiveness** is choosing to let full positive feelings toward the offending person return to your emotions. Ideally, this means to have and retain a feeling of value, love, and acceptance towards the offender. Any one of us can restore these feelings if and when we really desire it. The trouble is that most of the time we do not really want to restore and extend those positive feelings to the offending other person.

And of great additional importance, **True Forgiveness** does not mean that you are required to approve of the wrong treatment, emotions, and/or beliefs of the offending other, or to associate in any way with a toxic or predatory person who has done something wrong to you or who intends to do so. It just means that you choose to let yourself value that person as is rightfully due to any human being. Remember that **True Forgiveness** is a gift that is most often undeserved, but which is necessarily exercised for our own happiness. As long as we fail to choose forgiveness, we choose to have less happiness.

Choosing **True Forgiveness** sets us emotionally free from the person who has offended us, allows us to <u>fully forget</u> the offense, potentially improves the relationship and/or interactions with the offending other, and of course, eliminates any anger that we had towards that other person, thus increasing our personal happiness.

Chapter 9

My Promise to My Wife

How is he going to be able to keep this difficult promise?

In 2005, I was living in Seoul, South Korea and teaching university psychology courses to U.S. military members and their adult dependents. Fortunately for me, Debby, my best friend and wife of 34 years, was living there with me as often was our college-aged daughter, Abby, who came to visit and travel with us during the summers and Christmas holidays. As you might expect, the three of us had many fascinating experiences while we were in Korea and when we visited other Asian countries.

By that time in my life, I thought that I really understood a lot about human anger in general and my own anger issues in particular. Generally speaking, I felt that I had successfully learned how to be slow to anger, and to be mild in any anger that I did. But like many people, I still had various core emotional issues that almost always immediately triggered my anger programming.

Chapter 9: My Promise to My Wife

What was helpful for me in relation to my core emotional issues though, was that by that time in my life, I had already learned how we get programmed for anger early in our lives, and more importantly, how to significantly reduce anger as I have discussed earlier.

Additionally, and this is very important, I did not believe then, and I do not believe now that *suppressing* anger is healthy. Instead, I knew then that *reducing/eliminating* anger is a healthier and the correct choice to make.

Little did I know that my own core emotional issue/triggers would lead me to learn the most important psychological insight and vital key to human happiness that I have learned in the past 15 years of my life. Let me restate this for emphasis. I know a lot about psychology and about how to gain happiness, but the most important insight that I have gained in the past 15 years is how to **totally eliminate anger** from my life.

This is how it happened. Debby and I lived in Seoul, Korea about a 15 minute walk from the Yongsan U.S Army Post, and Abby was staying with us at that time. I had an early evening psychology course to teach on post, and so I left home in plenty of time to do a couple of errands and then easily walk to my class. When I got to the Yongsan Army Post, to my irritation, I found that I had forgotten some materials that I needed for my class that night.

Because my wife Debby and my daughter Abby were planning to come to the post later, and were still at our apartment, I called and asked Debby to find and bring the things that I needed, and to meet me on base before my class. Debby said that she was able to find what I had forgotten, and so we arranged to meet at a specific time at the post food court. I was glad that the help that I needed was convenient for her, because she had been planning to go shopping with Abby at the Post Exchange (PX) anyway.

At the appointed time, I went to the food court and searched for Debby and Abby. I did not find them, but to be sure that I had not somehow missed them, I looked carefully all through the food court rooms again. I was not worried, but because I really wanted my class materials, I called our apartment again. There was no answer, so I assumed that they were just a little delayed for some reason, but would soon arrive. So I waited, and waited, and waited.

As I waited, I was getting a bit irritated, and I thought that maybe, somehow, Debby must have misunderstood that I needed my materials at a certain time or misunderstood that we were to meet at the food court. This better thinking was part of my better anger reduction programming, and it was effective in reducing my irritation.

Again, doing some better thinking, I thought that perhaps Debby thought that we were to meet at the PX department store, so I walked to the nearby PX to look for her there. I carefully looked through the whole rather large PX, but with no success in locating Debby and Abby. At that point, it was almost time for my class to start, and so my initial irritation had accelerated to moderate anger.

Chapter 9: My Promise to My Wife

In that negative emotional condition, I immediately left the PX and went back to the food court. Once there, I rapidly searched the food court rooms again twice for Debby and Abby. But they were not there. During this unsuccessful and frustrating search, my core emotional issue anger programming was generating lots of negative thoughts about Debby and about my selfish interests being violated. And sadly, I did not have the maturity to reject those negative thoughts.

By this time, I had scaled up my negative anger emotions and thoughts to an 8 out of 10 on the anger scale. I felt that Debby had violated a core respect and responsibility emotional issue of mine, and after 34 years of marriage, she knew that was a sensitive core emotional issue for me.

Then, as I looked toward the PX, I thought I saw Debby and Abby casually walking toward the entrance of the PX. I could not believe it! I thought, "How could my wife be so irresponsible and uncaring about something so important to me?"

I quickly walked across the parking lot and caught up with them at the PX entrance. By the time we met, I had consciously ramped my anger back down to a 3 out of 10, so I felt reasonably pleased with my "mature" restraint in the face of the serious wrong that I felt my wife was inflicting on me.

When I got Debby's attention, she seemed to be totally unconcerned about the time, even though I was then late to teach my class. I scolded her for not being at the food court on time, got my materials from her, and left in a hurry for my class.

Several hours later when I returned home, I noticed that things were emotionally and conversationally "chilly". Perhaps you have experienced or created the "Arctic Chill" in one of your important relationships.

To my annoyance, Debby's behavior towards me continued that way for a couple of days. I thought to myself, "What is her problem? She is the one who committed the wrong and acted thoughtlessly. I am innocent of any wrongdoing. Why is she immaturely and wrongfully treating me this way?"

At last, after a couple of days of minimal to no positive communication, we arrived at the day and hour of "problem solving quality" communication. I do not remember who brought the issue up, but we both were reasonably able at that point to discuss with each other what had gone wrong and what to do about preventing it in the future.

As our communication session progressed, Debby emotionally and tearfully explained to me how embarrassing and humiliating my scolding of her in public and in front of our daughter had been. Oddly to me, she did not seem to realize how much her actions had hurt me. But despite that, I really wanted to understand her point of view and the emotional effect our emotional PX confrontation had on her.

Chapter 9: My Promise to My Wife

As I honestly listened to Debby, and considered in my heart how I had hurt her, I began to feel deep remorse for having hurt her. As I listened and understood about this, I mentally decided to say nothing about how she had violated a core emotional issue of mine, even though I deeply wanted her to understand and have her never repeat the violating behavior again.

I decided to give up my *false belief* that my wife should, after 34 years of marriage, understand how to respect all of my Core Emotional Issues (Chapter 1).

I did not and do not want to emotionally hurt my wife. I love her deeply. So I sincerely apologized for hurting her and asked her to forgive me. That is when I had my epiphany, my super insight, my great "ah-ha!" moment.

I am guessing that you probably want to know exactly what it is, but I will defer to Chapter 20, My Most Important Insight About Anger Elimination, to tell you exactly what I learned and about the wonderful personal change that you can make in your life by emotionally embracing that same insight. I know what you learn from that Chapter will give you lifelong benefits and a gigantic advantage towards fulfilling your personal happiness.

The conclusion of this true spousal relationship story is what I did next. Using the insight I had just gained, I made a very important and difficult to keep promise to Debby.

Chapter 9: My Promise to My Wife

I sincerely promised my wife that I would <u>NEVER</u> be angry with her again!

By this I meant I would not get angry at all or if I slipped and got angry, I would correct that privately and in a few minutes at the most.

To report on my progress with keeping this promise, over the years since 2005, I have had great success, but I have not been perfect in not getting angry at all. I have slipped into emotional auto pilot a few times in relation to my remaining core emotional issues. But those slips are rare (only a few times a year), mild in negative emotion (annoyed rather than angry), and of very short duration (a few minutes only instead of hours, days, or weeks). And at those times, I realize/know/accept that the problem is with me and not with her.

Chapter 10

Your Social Intuition & True Intuition/Insight

How to Better Understand, Accept, and Internalize the Anger Elimination Insights in This Book

  This Chapter is about the importance of learning to *"hear"* or *feel* and *follow* your **True Intuition** and question, revise, or reject your **Social Intuition** as it relates to your anger and your expectations of others.

  Intuition is not very well researched or understood by the vast majority of psychologists or by the vast majority of people in general. It is often described as a "gut feeling" that something is true or false, right or wrong, or good or bad. All of the world's cultures have some sort of term for intuition because it is commonly experienced by almost everyone in every culture. True intuition is vital to successful and happy life, and another common term for it in Western cultures is **Insight**.

I have found, through much observation and much personal research, that all mentally and emotionally accountable human beings, perhaps in many cases excluding those who are severely retarded, severely brain damaged, and in all cases those who are 100% sociopaths, have the gift or ability of true intuition.

This is not to be confused with the "intuition" that most psychologists study and discuss. To be helpful, I will refer to that as **Social Intuition**, which is based on our flawed or limited past experiences, beliefs, unconscious memories, and emotions (our program).

Unfortunately, most people do not have a very good understanding of how they are being continually influenced by true intuition/insight and social intuition. Hopefully the following information will help you to understand both types of intuition better.

Social intuition, that which most psychologists just refer to as intuition, is reasonably described as the massive amount of personal unconscious memories or habituated mental and emotional programming which each of us is influenced by at all times. It is established and shaped by such things as our choices, our family interaction, the media, our peer associations, our strong positive and negative life experiences, our cultural influences, our individual education, and all other life experiences and associations.

Because all of our vast past experiences, and the information, beliefs, and emotions which they are

Chapter 10: Your Social Intuition & True Intuition

based on, or are associated with, are recorded or programmed in our unconscious, we generally do not realize how those things are always influencing us.

Although most of us are not consciously aware of it, we always experience automatic mild positive or negative emotional reactions to new things, situations, and/or people. And at times we experience strong automatic positive or negative emotional reactions ("gut feelings") when we experience something new, encounter some new situation, or meet some new person. These feelings, which are based on our programming, always influence what we think, believe, and do. They are our social intuition feelings.

In general, we have little interest or ability to analyze those program generated feelings for truth and usefulness. That being so, the difficulty is that social intuitive feelings are at times totally correct/important/useful, are at time varied mixtures of correct and incorrect influence, and are at times quite or totally wrong.

The usefulness or harm to us from our social intuitive feelings, depends on the accuracy and completeness of our perceptions of past experiences upon which they are based. And upon how closely the current experience matches the essential elements of the past experience, which is triggering our automated social intuitive feelings.

On the other hand, **True Intuition/Insight** is never wrong, and I really do mean *never*. We all have and experience the guidance of true intuition to a greater or lesser degree throughout our lives. It gives us accurate guidance in every aspect of our lives, no matter how small or unimportant that aspect may seem or be. One way to describe this universal human attribute is to call it our access to the database of all that is true.

Every world culture recognizes the operation of true intuition/insight to some degree, but they give it different names and attribute it to different sources according to their cultural traditions preferences. Some call it conscience, some call it collective unconscious, some call it guidance from Deity/God, some call it ancestral memory, some call it the universal intelligence, and so forth.

It is important to note here that **Insight** and **True Intuition** are the same thing. Every positive advancement that has ever been made, and that is currently being made in human life, has involved the necessary guidance referred to as insight. This necessary guidance from insight that has been and is experienced by individuals who are discovering good things, who are improving things in innovative ways, who are inventing useful things, who are correcting previous wrongs in important ways, is spoken of and is recorded in many ways and in many places.

When someone carefully studies large and small historical improvements or advancements in any world culture, and/or the current ones, he or she can always encounter the observed and/or recorded influence of insight as it has helped things to be better for the people involved.

Chapter 10: Your Social Intuition & True Intuition

What is most important, and as I said before, true intuition/insight is never wrong. It warns us when we are heading for emotional, behavioral, or thinking errors of commission or omission. And, it quietly confirms to us when our commission or omission of emotions, thoughts, beliefs, and behaviors are appropriate or correct.

Accordingly, it is vital that we learn how to use true intuition more frequently in our decision making and interactions with others. It is also vital to learn how to increase our ability to discern and recognize its messages in our thoughts and feelings.

It is certainly tricky to accurately separate what is the guidance and influence of our social intuition from what is the guidance and influence of our true intuition. Fortunately, with a desire to understand we can learn to do this better and better with concerted and continual conscious practice.

Most of us have a problem with understanding and noticing the difference between our social intuition and our true intuition, once we realize that both of them are always acting to influence our thoughts, beliefs, emotions, and behaviors. To help us overcome that problem, it is important to know that true intuition is almost always in the form of very *"quiet"* or gentle messages to our thoughts and feelings, and our flawed and incomplete social intuition, which is based on unconscious thoughts, beliefs, and feelings in our individual program, is almost always in the form of very *"loud"* messages to our thoughts and feelings.

What this means is that usually our thoughts about various things are constantly going through our minds, and our emotions about what we are experiencing in our lives are often being strongly expressed and felt. In other words, often, our thoughts are congested and our feelings are noisy.

It is very important to learn how to be much "quieter" in thought and emotion, in order to correctly discern or "hear" our true intuition messages and guidance. Because true intuition is gentle or "quiet", we often cannot "hear", feel, or discern it, because our "loud" thoughts and feelings drown it out. In order to "hear", feel, or discern true intuition better, it is vital to open and clear or pause your thoughts, and to calm your emotions. When you do that, hopefully on an increasing basis, you will be much more aware of and benefitted by true intuitive/insight guidance.

Another problem that we have in recognizing information from true intuition, is that often what true intuition communicates to us, seems to be contrary to reason, what we believe to be true, or what we have previously experienced. Consequently, we do not follow the correct guidance that it gives us. In those cases, it is our rigidly held, wrong, or incomplete beliefs that are keeping us from properly recognizing, discerning, and being helped by the true intuition/insight guidance.

Our ability to receive and "hear" true intuitive guidance is directly related to our willingness to receive and follow its guidance. The more willing we are to follow its guidance, meaning that we believe what it is communicating

Chapter 10: Your Social Intuition & True Intuition

to us, we act when it suggests acting, or do not act if it suggests not acting, the clearer its guidance becomes to us. The opposite is true when we reject/ignore its guidance.

Each time we reject or ignore the correct guidance from true intuition, that makes it harder for us to "hear" or feel its guidance the next time. If we continually reject its directions about any given topic, true intuition becomes harder and harder to "hear", feel, or discern, until we cannot "hear" or feel it at all about that topic.

When we have chosen or decided on some course of action or inaction in thought, belief, emotion, or behavior, true intuition always clearly signals us that our choice is good, bad, or mixed by quiet thoughts and feelings which occur to us and which we can "hear", feel, or discern. Of course, this guidance is most helpful if we take the time to listen for or feel that guidance before we act on our decision.

Now, you may be wondering why I have included this chapter in a book about anger elimination. Call it a special bonus. The information in this chapter will lead you to a greater level of successful living. I have included it because you can use your true intuition guidance to evaluate what I have written in this book about anger. That will help you to understand what I have written better and to know that what I am sharing with you is indeed very valuable to you, to those you associate with, and to those that you know well and love. Of course, you may already understand these things, and if so, very good!

Chapter 10: Your Social Intuition & True Intuition

The next chapter describes a real anger experience involving the violation of 8 core emotional issues. That anger experience occurred in a professional work setting, and it demonstrates how anger damaged the individual involved over a long period of time.

Chapter 11

Andy's Anger At Work

8 Core Emotional Issues Violated and Their "Cost" to Andy

This true anger story is about Andy and his anger-inducing or triggering working conditions. The educational organization where he worked was below average in terms of quality of organizational culture, meaning that the standard for the organization was to generally disregard the well being of its employees. This negativity of organizational culture was manifested in many ways, including poor leadership, a punitive motivational system, below average wages, little or no recognition for quality work done, deceptive communications by supervisors/executives to employees, and few work enhancing resources provided for key employees like Andy.

There are potentially eight core emotional issues (Chapter 1) that were abused or violated in this work situation. Each of which usually stimulates strong anger in the recipient of the related violation of the core emotional issue. As you read through the following story, try to identify these violations.

Andy was a psychology professor, and Lena was the director of services for his academic area and so she was his administrative supervisor. Andy had a very good reputation in the organization for providing quality education, helping the students, and readily building the organization in many ways without expectation of compensation or recognition. He was very popular with the students and was well liked by the administrative staff of his university.

One day after teaching class, Andy was asked by a student to advise her about some important matters. His job description required that he advised students as requested, but he did not have a private office to do advising in, because of the low quality of his organization's culture. So, he arranged with a staff member to use a common room in his university's building, which was by the administrative office.

Andy arranged to use the common room for the hour required to meet with the student. He was careful to be sure that his use of the common room would not be problematic for anyone else. Then, as he was entering the room with the student and before he closed the door, he was greeted by Lena who happened to be passing in the hallway. After a brief exchange, Andy closed the door and advised the student for an hour, concluding with the student being very pleased with the results of the discussion.

Chapter 11: Andy's Anger At Work

And as you probably realize already, Andy felt very good about having been able to help the student resolve her issues.

A few days later, Andy received an e-mail from Lena, who without any explanation, informed him that he would not be required to teach classes during the summer term although he had successfully done so for several previous years, and there was a need for the classes to be taught. Lena also asked him to explain what he was doing in the common room behind a closed door with a student.

Andy was disappointed by the news of not being wanted as a summer term instructor, but based on several years of experience with his organization, he thought it typical of the low quality culture of his organization, and was not upset about the change in his teaching expectations. On the other hand, he was troubled by Lena's request to know more about his advisement session with the student.

Being an ethical person, a willing helper for students who needed his help, and a respecter of the student's privacy, Andy knew that he was acting within his normal job description and that he should not be questioned about such a routine advising session.

Due to the oddness of the e-mail from Lena, Andy discussed it with his wife to try to understand how to best answer the inquiry. They concluded that it would be best to respond to the e-mail and ask for clarification about the "not being required to teach classes in the summer term" part of the e-mail and to ignore the other part, because they felt it was inappropriate to divulge the private details of his meeting with the student without her permission to do so. Consequently, that is what Andy did.

A few days later, Andy got a second e-mail from Lena which stated that he would not be teaching any classes during the summer term, and which asked again about the meeting with the student. Andy was disturbed that he was again asked inappropriately about the advising meeting with the student. He discussed the matter again with his wife, and they decided that it would be best to again ignore Lena's request for more information hoping that Lena would realize on her own that her request was inappropriate and even abusive.

After several more days, Andy got a telephone message from the organization's EEOC office requesting a discussion about a concern that someone had about Andy's behavior. When Andy returned the call, he learned that Lena had filed a formal concern about his advising meeting with the student based on the assumption that their meeting included inappropriate sexual harassment involving the student.

At that point, Andy got very angry. He stated that he was very offended by the assumption of any wrong doing on his part, and, he knew that he was morally, professionally, and legally bound to respect the student's privacy. He said that the student requested the meeting and that he would not discuss it with others without the permission of the student.

Chapter 11: Andy's Anger At Work 81

At the conclusion of this conversation, Andy told the EEOC staff member that he required and expected an apology from Lena.

After finishing this EEOC telephone discussion, Andy found that he was furious that his moral integrity was in question. He shared his feelings with his wife which resulted in her also becoming angry. She was angry because she felt irreparable harm had been done to her husband's moral reputation. After a few hours, Andy got to a point where he could let go of his anger, but his wife was understandably unable to let go of hers for several days.

Soon, instead of the appropriate apology from Lena, Andy got a final e-mail which scolded him for using a common room, even though he had appropriate permission, and instructed him to never talk with a student in private again, so as to avoid any appearance of impropriety. Needless to say, Andy and his wife got angry all over again. They had a variety of *false beliefs* about Lena's maturity and level of professionalism, and *false expectations* about being appropriately treated and respected by an administrator who should have had the maturity to do so.

At the beginning of this account, I mentioned that there were potentially eight Core Emotional Issues that were abused or violated in this work situation. The violated Core Emotional Issues for Andy and his wife were:

Threat to personal worth and/or reputation:
Lena's unwarranted EEOC complaint against Andy

Being financially abused: Andy's loss of summer employment

Gender prejudice and/or discrimination: Lena's false assumption that Andy's behavior was inappropriate because he was a man.

Disrespect: Lena's refusal to apologize for her wrong and hurtful opinions and communications

Violation of trust by a person in authority: Andy and his wife had wrongfully trusted Lena to treat Andy with the respect that he truly deserved

A friend, loved one, or innocent being threatened, harmed, or abused: Andy's wife's reaction to the harm done to Andy

Being emotionally bullied: Lena's relentless harassment of Andy based on a very false assumption

Petty abuse of power: Lena complaint against Andy to the EEOC and wrongful instruction about his advising responsibilities

Perhaps you are saying to yourself, Andy's and his wife's anger was typical and justified. And, I would agree with you, but I have found that even though their anger responses might have been expected and warranted, the anger was too costly for them mentally and emotionally, as well as in attitude and time "cost".

Chapter 11: Andy's Anger At Work

The mental cost for Andy was the many hours that he spent thinking about how to respond so he could "put Lena in her place", end the abuse, and restore his wrongfully damaged reputation. He thought seriously about, but ended up deciding not to pursue legal action against Lena, although at first he really, really wanted to make her suffer some consequence for her hurtful behavior. Andy's wife also spent much of her emotional energy stressing and fuming about the offenses, and she spent much of her mental energy and time thinking about this situation and how to deal effectively with Lena's wrong assumptions, attitudes, and behaviors.

The emotional cost to Andy and his wife was the loss of their happiness for days. The cost in attitude for them was a greatly diminished respect for the education organization and its administrators, and the cost in time for them both was that they could have spent their time in much more productive and happy ways, rather than by wasting it in angry thoughts and emotions.

Anger in this example was "justified", but was not worth what it "cost" Andy and his wife!

Chapter 12

Thoughts & Beliefs "Create" Emotions

How Thoughts, Beliefs, Emotions, Behaviors, Biology, and Environment Mutually Change Each Other

As I have discussed in The Great & Dreadful Anger Path (Chapter 6), in Reducing Anger by Replacing Your Anger Habits (Chapter 7), and have referred to in several other chapters, thoughts and beliefs "create" your emotional responses.

The reason that I have placed quotation marks around the word "create" is because while we are born with the ability to engage/activate the psychological and biological elements of emotions, we learn/experience, and thus program into our unconscious, the specific connections between our negative and positive emotions and a vast number of things, words, situations, attitudes, and people. Those emotionally

Chapter 12: Thoughts & Beliefs "Create" Emotions

connected unconscious memories about things, words, situations, attitudes, and people in our unconscious/program, are our automatic triggers for all of our positive and negative mental, emotional, and physiological emotional reactions.

Then when we consciously think about those preprogrammed emotion triggers or even related ones, our beliefs about them are activated, and we experience the related programmed emotions. As a result, our thoughts and beliefs "create" or activate our emotions.

If you believe that you have no hope of forming a successful romantic relationship with someone, that belief and its related negative thoughts will active the emotion of sadness, depression, or even anger. If you believe that your boss does not like you and that he or she is going to give you a bad performance evaluation leading to your firing because of his or her personal feelings about you, that belief and its related negative thoughts will activate anxiety, fear, depression, and probably anger as well as less positive and productive behaviors.

If you believe that your upcoming two week vacation at the beach, mountains, or a resort will be a wonderful experience for you and your loved ones, that belief and its associated positive thoughts will activate such emotions as hope, joy, relief, happiness, anticipation, and gratitude. If you believe that the quality restaurant meal that you just ate was delicious, that belief and its associated thoughts will activate such emotions as satisfaction, generosity, gratitude, and happiness.

Chapter 12: Thoughts & Beliefs "Create" Emotions

Thoughts and beliefs, emotions and motivations, behaviors, biology, and environment are all mutually interactive. I often use the following diagram to illustrate this relationship.

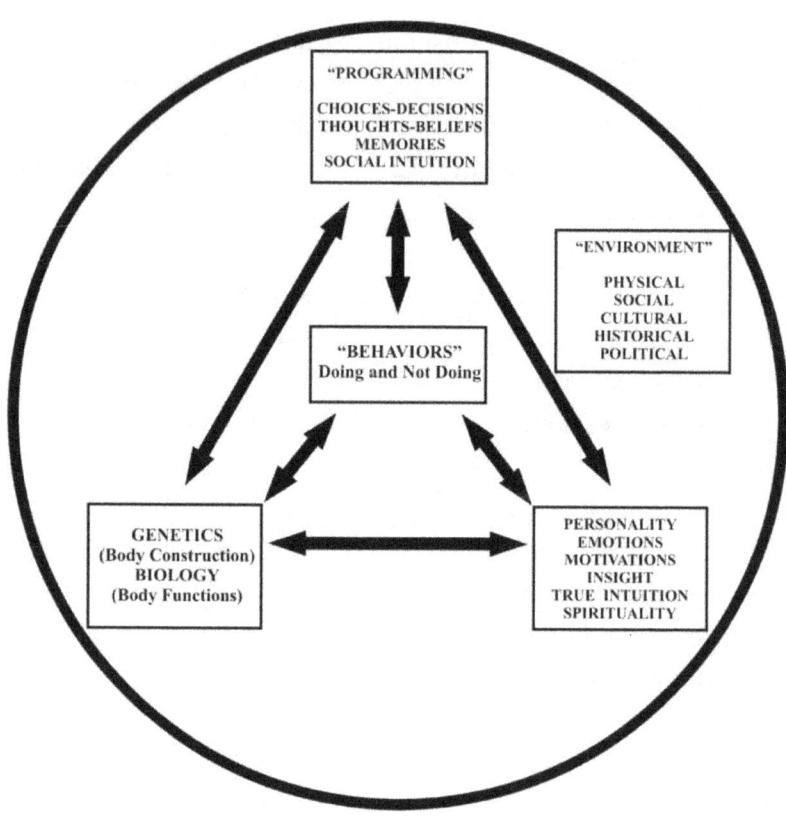

As you can see from the diagram above, Thoughts and beliefs, emotions and motivations, behaviors, and biology each can be and **always** are influenced by each other. This is because none of these human factors are really separate from the others. In addition, the circle represents

Chapter 12: Thoughts & Beliefs "Create" Emotions

that you are continually surrounded by and influenced by things external to you. These are "environmental" factors of all kinds. And whatever is the current condition of your thoughts and beliefs, emotions and motivations, behaviors, and biology, those parts of you always affect the "environments" that you seek and interact with.

At this point, you may wish to read or reread the following chapters, so that you can see the application of what has been presented in this chapter:

Chapter 3: Brian's Anger Issues

Chapter 6: The Great & Dreadful Anger Path

Chapter 9: My Promise to My Wife

Chapter 11: Andy's Anger at Work

Chapter 16: Ellen's Anger at Graduate School

Chapter 18: Roger's Anger Over the Years

When you read these Chapters, try to identify the anger activating thoughts and beliefs related to the Core Emotional Issues (Chapter 1) of these individuals. You may also wish to recall when your own Core Emotional Issues have been violated, and the thoughts and beliefs that you had or still have that activate your own anger emotions.

As you will read about in My Most Important Insight About Anger Elimination (Chapter 20), it is the informed, conscious, and emotionally committed replacement of your ***false beliefs*** and associated ***false thoughts*** that is required in order for you to mentally master and reprogram your emotions, and thus eliminate anger and gain greater happiness.

Chapter 13

The Four Sources of Thoughts

Thoughts: the good, the bad, the neutral, the trivial, the beautiful, and the ugly

I am including this chapter in part to help you understand what influences the Anger Path (Chapter 6) in negative ways. What you learn in this chapter may also help you come to healthier terms with the "good", "bad", "beautiful", and "ugly" thoughts that occur to you on a regular basis.

You may or may not agree with what I have to say about this topic. But whether you agree or not, do consider that I have seriously studied about the sources of human though from various perspectives over many years of my adult life both as a person living life and as a reasonably good scientist. And so, I am not including this chapter frivolously.

So, please do consider being a good "scientist" yourself, and as you live your life, look for data/information that is related to what I present in this chapter. That will help you evaluate the practical value of what I have to say.

The **Four Sources of our Thoughts** are:

- Thoughts that we consciously generate ourselves or that are part of our unconscious programming and are automatically triggered by various stimuli. These can be good, bad, neutral, trivial, beautiful, or ugly;
- Thoughts which originate from others that we at times believe to be our own thoughts and at times that we recognize are thoughts coming from someone else;
- Negative (Bad, Ugly) External Thoughts, which originate from a negative external source that is destructive to us and our happiness. We most often believe these thoughts to be our own thoughts; and
- Positive (Good, Beautiful) External Thoughts, which originate from a positive external source that is constructive to us and our happiness. We most often believe these thoughts to be our own thoughts.

I have listed these sources of our thoughts in the following order. First, what a person would consider as common and reasonable knowledge about our thoughts. Second, what a person might consider as a possible source of our thoughts. And finally what many people would consider as "Twilight Zone" or fantasy information (but it is true).

Chapter 13: The Four Sources of Thoughts

The **first source of thoughts**, are thoughts which we consciously generate ourselves, or that are part of our unconscious program, is the source of our thoughts that most people believe is the source of all of their thoughts. Simply put, this is not the only source of thoughts that occur to us throughout our lives.

Perhaps obviously, we can choose to think about anything that we have some experience or memory about, we can allow ourselves to follow one thought as it lead to another thought, and we can formulate new thoughts as we have new experiences and when we choose to be inventive, imaginative, or creative. All of our use of this first (and maybe most important) source of our thoughts, can lead us to various sorts of advances in understanding and experience or to various sorts of negative outcomes in us and in our lives.

Thoughts that we personally generate can be neutral in nature, can be harmful to us and others, and can be beneficial to us and others. The good thing here is that we have a high personal control potential in relation to these thoughts, in that we can choose what we will think about, when we will think about it, and how we will think about it.

The **second source of thoughts**, are thoughts which originate from others that we at times believe to be our own thoughts, and at other times that we recognize are thoughts coming from someone else. As strange as it may sound, we humans do have the ability to a greater or to a lesser degree, to somehow tap into another person's thoughts.

You may totally reject this reality, but there is ample historical and current data that supports it, and there are a lot of us that tap into others thoughts on a regular basis without consciously realizing that we are doing it.

I really do not know how this is accomplished, but I do know from personal experience that a person can develop this ability that is probably inherent in all of us. Because most of us, most of the time, are operating on "autopilot" we naturally may fail to recognize that we are tuned in to someone else's thoughts at all. I have observed this as a well developed ability which is found frequently and widely in caring parents, close friends, quality teachers, caring mentors, insightful counselors, quality organizational leaders, and loving couples.

In all likelihood, about 16% of the general population are pretty good at tuning in to others' thoughts, although as I said before, most of them probably do not even realize that they are tuned in to someone else's thoughts. Mostly they probably believe that they are good readers of non-verbal messages, between-the-lines verbal content, and so forth, if they think about this at all.

The reason that I am willing to include this source of thoughts, in this chapter's discussion, is that I personally have known and interacted with various individuals who are very good at knowing others' thoughts. And, I know of many others, through my study of their lives and writings, who are/were also very good at tapping into others' thoughts.

Chapter 13: The Four Sources of Thoughts

Some of these men and women are exceedingly good at this ability. And, although I am not great at tuning in to others' thoughts myself, I have personally been able to develop my own latent abilities to do this somewhat better myself, on an appropriate need to know basis.

The **third source of thoughts** that I have included in this chapter is Negative (Bad, Ugly) External Thoughts, which originate from a negative external source that is actively destructive to us and our happiness. We most often believe these thoughts to be our own thoughts.

This source of these negative thoughts is external to any part of us, meaning that these thoughts are not ours, even thought we almost always believe that they are ours. Obviously, I am not able to demonstrate the truth of this to you or verify it scientifically, but I do know from much personal study and observation, that it is true.

Our various world cultures have different ideas about, and ways of, describing what the source of negative external thoughts is, and if you choose to study this topic further, you will find that virtually all of our world cultures have an acceptance and representations of this reality in some aspects of their cultures. In many cultures the negative external thoughts are believed to be temptations (to do, think, believe, or feel something wrong), which when accepted prevent positive personal development (e.g. from an evil unseen person/being or persons/beings).

In other world cultures, the negative external thoughts are believed to be the necessary and natural balance (e.g. yin/yang) to positive external thoughts, each defining the other by opposition, and providing a condition which allows us to freely choose what we want to do, think, believe, and feel.

It seems that thoughts of this nature (negative, destructive, harmful, ugly) are continually being presented to our minds in a form that causes us to accept the thoughts as our own, and to not notice that an external source is providing them. If we were to realize that these thoughts are not our thoughts, and that they are harmful to us and others, we would of course quickly reject them or not pay any attention to them at all.

The **fourth source of thoughts** that I have included in this chapter is Positive External Thoughts. Unlike the third source of thoughts, these thoughts originate from a source that is actively benevolent to us and our happiness. And just like our reaction to the negative external source of thoughts, most of us also believe that these positive external thoughts are our own thoughts. As I said before, I am not able to demonstrate the truth of this positive external source of thoughts to you, or verify it scientifically, but I do know from much personal study and observation, that it is true.

As is true for negative external thoughts, our various world cultures have different ideas about, and ways of describing what the source of positive external thoughts is.

Chapter 13: The Four Sources of Thoughts

And if you choose to study this topic further, you will find that virtually all of our world cultures have an acceptance and representation of this reality in some aspects of their cultures. In many cultures the Positive External Thoughts are believed to be inspirations or encouragements (to do, think, believe, or feel something right or good), which when accepted, facilitate positive personal development for self and others.

Many world cultures believe that this source of external thoughts originates from a benevolent unseen person/being or persons/beings (e.g. God, angels, benevolent ancestors, positive life forces, collective unconscious, etc). And as I said before, in other cultures, the Positive External Thoughts are believed to be the necessary and natural balance (e.g. yin/yang) to Negative External Thoughts, each defining the other by opposition, and providing a condition which allows us to freely choose what we want to do, think, believe, and feel.

It seems that thoughts of this nature (positive, uplifting, comforting, healing, inspiring) are continually being presented to our minds in a form that allows us to accept the thoughts as our own and to not notice that an external source is providing them. If we were to always realize that these thoughts are not our thoughts, but that they are always good, we would quickly cease to be able to make unbiased choices in our lives and so fail to learn for ourselves what we value most.

The next chapter presents some good information about where to live and where to avoid living if you want to live around and associate with fewer angry people or less angry people. The correlational research studies that the next chapter's information are based on, measured various important life variables which are highly related to triggering our anger reactions.

Based on the results of those studies, and additional anger correlates, it may be time for you to help improve the conditions in the city or area where you live, or it may be time for you to move to a better city or area!

Chapter 14

Anger Cities

Anger triggers/conditions which may be better or worse in the city or area where you live

An interesting bit of correlational research by Matt Marion (2008) which was published in an online article from the magazine <u>Men's Health</u>, found that 100 major cities in the United States could be ranked in terms of the probability of more or less anger among their residents. This research identified factors that correlate with anger and then ranked 100 major cities in the United States in terms of potential anger levels in each.

The anger research factors that were selected for their correlation with anger were (1) Traffic Congestion Conditions from the Texas Transportation Institute (traffic congestion is correlated with Road Rage); (2) FBI compiled rates of aggravated assault; (3) U.S. Bureau of Labor statistics on reported violence/assaults resulting in death in the workplaces across the country; (4) Speeding Citations statistics compiled by the Governors Highway Safety Association; and (5) National data about the percentage of American males having higher blood pressure, which the researchers obtained from Sperling's BestPlaces calculations involving data from the U.S. Center for Disease Control's Behavioral Risk Factor Surveillance System.

A second article about an anger city study was published in the magazine Men's Health in 2011, using most of the same correlation variables used in the 2008 study

You may well recognize that the correlational factors of the above mentioned 2 research studies have not been **proven** to cause anger, but they are reasonably related to or associated with anger. You may also notice, as you consider the following ranked list of major American cities, that some states have more or less cities with higher anger probability as compared to other states. Some of the difference in number of anger cities in a given state is due to the state's population density and some is due to differences in the presence and severity of potential anger correlated variables listed later in this chapter.

There are all sorts of potential reasons for the differences between states and cities in the states, in potential anger of its citizens. Those **potential reasons** for state differences in having more or less cities with high or low anger potentials could involve any or all of the following anger correlated or triggering variables.

Chapter 14: Anger Cities

(1) population density;

(2) poverty levels;

(3) average positive moral level;

(4) ethnic diversity;

(5) amount of substance abuse;

(6) the political mix and attitudes;

(7) cultural history of its residents;

(8) conditions that make it easier/harder for people with marginal personal emotional maturity to live/survive;

(9) attitudes toward personal or ethnic entitlement;

(10) ignorance and education levels;

(11) selfishness levels;

(12) percentage of recent emigrants;

(13) amount of unemployment;

(14) temperature fluctuations and discomfort;

(15) frequency and severity of natural disasters;

(16) strictness of reporting of anger correlates;

(17) effectiveness of law enforcement;

(18) quality of family life;

(19) existing effective aggression deterrent laws;

(20) religious attitudes and behaviors;

(21) political corruption;

(22) citizen apathy;

(23) large socio-economic differences;

(24) demographic distribution, etc.;

(25) per capita violent physical assaults and rapes;

(26) quality of infrastructure and environment;

(27) stress levels;

(28) level and quality of social support services;

(29) per capita counselors specializing in anger reduction;

(30) amount of bullying;

(31) prevalence of manners and civility;

(32) conditions in the surrounding suburban and rural areas;

Chapter 14: Anger Cities

Listed next are the potential anger rankings of 100 major American cities ranked from most anger potential (1) to least anger potential (100). The data is from both the 2008 and the 2011 studies (Men's Health, Marion, 2008) (Men' Health, 2011).

In the data boxes/cells of the following anger data tables, the first city listed in each box/cell is from the anger ranking in 2008, and the second city listed in each box/cell is from the anger ranking in 2011.

By 2011, some cities have gotten worse and some have gotten better in relation to the potential anger correlates measured. And by now (2016), there are probably additional meaningful negative and positive changes. It would be good to know what was mostly responsible for the negative and positive changes in your city or area and if those efforts and influences are continuing.

Time to get busy helping things get better or time to move?

1	Orlando, FL/ Detroit, MI	26	Denver, CO/ Sacramento, CA
2	St. Petersburg, FL/ Baltimore, MD	27	Philadelphia, PA/ Washington, DC
3	Detroit, MI/ St. Petersburg, FL	28	Baton Rouge, LA/ St. Louis, MO
4	Baltimore, MD/ Las Vegas, NV	29	Fort Worth, TX/ Phoenix, AZ
5	Nashville, TN/ Newark, NJ	30	Phoenix, AZ/ Baton Rouge, LA
6	Wilmington, DE/ Charleston, WV	31	Lubbock, TX/ San Jose, CA
7	Miami, FL/ Dallas, TX	32	Cleveland, OH/ Tampa, FL
8	Memphis, TN/ Houston, TX	33	Greensboro, NC/ Aurora, CO
9	Jacksonville, FL/ Philadelphia, PA	34	Cincinnati, OH/ El Paso, TX
10	St. Louis, MO/ Miami, FL	35	Arlington, TX/ Winston-Salem, NC
11	Chicago, IL/ Riverside, CA	36	Los Angeles, CA/ Birmingham, AL
12	Tampa, FL/ Memphis, TN	37	Buffalo, NY/ Tucson, AZ
13	Jackson, MS/ Oklahoma City, OK	38	Grand Rapids, MI/ Santa Ana, CA
14	Albuquerque, NM/ Louisville, KY	39	Boston, MA/ Bridgeport, CT
15	Charlotte, NC/ Los Angeles, CA	40	Columbia, SC/ Billings, MT
16	Dallas, TX/ Jersey City, NJ	41	Tulsa, OK/ Tulsa, OK
17	Houston, TX/ Fort Worth, TX	42	Aurora, CO/ Manchester, NH
18	Tucson, AZ/ Jacksonville, FL	43	Seattle, WA/ New York, NY
19	Indianapolis, IN/ Indianapolis, IN	44	Sacramento, CA/ Lexington, KY
20	Wichita, KS/ Boston, MA	45	San Diego, CA/ Little Rock, AR
21	Birmingham, AL/ Chicago, IL	46	Montgomery, AL/ St. Paul, MN
22	Providence, RI/ Orlando, FL	47	Raleigh, NC/ Charlotte, NC
23	Durham, NC/ New Orleans, LA	48	Yonkers, NY/ San Diego, CA
24	Atlanta, GA/ Stockton, CA	49	Oakland, CA/ Fresno, CA
25	Washington, DC/ Oakland, CA	50	Fort Wayne, IN/ Atlanta, GA

51	Newark, NJ/ Cleveland, OH	76	Hartford, CT/ Minneapolis, MN
52	Las Vegas, NV/ Columbus, OH	77	Minneapolis, MN/ Norfolk, VA
53	Columbus, OH/ Lubbock, TX	78	Boise, ID/ Honolulu, HI
54	St. Paul, MN/ San Antonio, TX	79	Anaheim, CA/ Wilmington, DE
55	Charleston, WV/ Plano, TX	80	Norfolk, VA/ Durham, NC
56	Kansas City, MO/ Richmond, VA	81	Austin, TX/ Seattle, WA
57	New York, NY/ Greensboro, NC	82	Fremont, CA/ Des Moines, IA
58	Oklahoma, OK/ Providence, RI	83	Fresno, CA/ Fort Wayne, IN
59	Toledo, OH/ Albuquerque, NM	84	Anchorage, AK/ Pittsburgh, PA
60	San Antonio, TX/ Denver, CO	85	Cheyenne, WY/ Boise, ID
61	Riverside, CA/ Austin, TX	86	Rochester, NY/ Omaha, NE
62	Modesto, CA/ Kansas City, MO	87	Madison, WI/ Portland, ME
63	Louisville, KY/ Jackson, MS	88	Salt Lake C UT/Virginia Beach VA
64	Honolulu, HI/ Bakersfield, CA	89	Omaha, NE/ Portland, OR
65	Richmond, VA/ Milwaukee, WI	90	Pittsburgh, PA/ Columbia, SC
66	San Francisco CA/San Francisco CA	91	Col. Springs, CO/ Anchorage, AK
67	Bakersfield, CA/ Chesapeake, VA	92	El Paso, TX/ Reno, NV
68	Spokane, WA/ Corpus Christi, TX	93	Sioux Falls, SD/ Wichita, KS
69	Milwaukee, WI/ Nashville, TN	94	Des Moines, IA/ Cheyenne, WY
70	Jersey City, NJ/ Sioux Falls, SD	95	Burlington, VT/ Salt Lake City, UT
71	Lexington, KY/ Raleigh, NC	96	Portland, OR/ Madison, WI
72	Little Rock, AR/ Toledo, OH	97	Corpus Christi TX/Col. Springs CO
73	Lincoln, NE/ Laredo, TX	98	Fargo, ND/ Fargo, ND
74	Billings, MT/ Cincinnati, OH	99	Bangor, ME/ Lincoln, NE
75	San Jose, CA/ Buffalo, NY	100	Manchester, NH/ Burlington, VT

Chapter 15

Gender & Other Anger Differences

Gender, Age, Socio-Economic Status (SES), and Ethnicity

When, why, how, and how much anger is stimulated or triggered and/or expressed, is strongly influenced by some combination of the gender, age, socio-economic status, and ethnicity of the individual or individuals involved. Knowing about the differences can help you understand your and others' anger triggers and expressions. This can also help you to eliminate your anger.

Gender Anger Differences

First of all, let me observe that men and women are much more alike than they are different. However, the diverse cultures of the world have culturally shaped their male and female members somewhat differently in relation

Chapter 15: Anger Differences

to what triggers anger, how strongly anger is triggered, and in what form anger expression is allowed, for each gender.

I have widely observed that men and women get angry differently about Core Emotional Issues (Chapter 1). I believe the most basic reasons for this are that, for whatever reason, most women generally are more nurturing, more concerned about relationships, more willing to apply mercy instead of justice, more willing to reveal emotional pain, more cooperative, and more tolerant of others mistakes.

I have also observed that women are generally more covert or concealed about their anger and so are more likely to express it through passive aggression. They seem to experience a lot of their anger as a slow, long lasting emotional burn.

On the other hand, I have observed that men are generally more competitive, more material goal oriented, less willing to forgo justice in favor of mercy, more overt in their expressions of anger, less willing to reveal emotional pain, and less nurturing. They are also generally allowed by their cultures to be more overt and physical in expressing their anger. Most men seem to experience a lot of their anger as a fast and hot flare up which dissipates or is mostly burned out after some sort of open aggression.

In relation to the 20 Core Emotional Issues, which are our hot-buttons for anger, women in general are most likely to get *strongly* angry about and generate the strongest feelings of anger regarding the following six particular core emotional issues. They are the Core Emotional Issues that are the ones most closely related to relationships.

6. Violation of Trust

8. Broken promises

9. Being physically, verbally, financially, sexually, or emotionally abused, bullied or cheated

10. A friend, a loved one, a helpless person, or an innocent person being threatened, harmed, or abused

12. Being denied something that is very important to you

15. Dishonoring or ignoring of requests, guidance, or instructions given to a subordinate or one's children, and the same neglect or opposition from one's spouse or coworker, when fulfillment of the requests, guidance, or instructions is appropriate

Women in general are *moderately* likely to get angry about these next five Core Emotional Issues.

13. Someone wrongfully taking credit for your plan, idea, or achievement

16. Passive or active "sabotage", delay, or blockage, by someone, of an idea, a solution, an objective, a task, a communication, or a project that is important to you

17. Anything that you consider to be meaningfully unjust or unfair

18. Anything (other than a person) that frustrates, hinders, or blocks something important to you

20. Someone identifying, pointing out, or telling you about your <u>true</u> faults, weaknesses, failings, wrong behaviors, etc.

Women in general are *less* likely to get angry or generate strong anger about the following nine Core Emotional Issues, but they are quite likely to feel emotionally hurt.

1. A personal moral or ethical trait, attribute, or strength being questioned or not believed

2. Being used, tricked, lied to, or deceived by someone

3. Disrespect toward you, a friend, or loved one

4. Being strongly devalued by someone

5. Prejudice and Discrimination

7. Abuse of Authority or Power

11. Property Issues--your property being carelessly damaged or lost or being purposefully damaged or stolen

14. Personal failure in something that is very important to you

19. Abuse of your time

On the other hand, men are *most* likely to get angry about the following 14 Core Emotional Issues and to generate the *strongest* anger regarding them. Almost all of these Core Emotional Issues have to do with justice violations, competition, masking emotional pain by converting it to anger, and others' negative opinions about a man's personal worth.

1. A personal moral or ethical trait, attribute, or strength being questioned or not believed

2. Being used, tricked, lied to, or deceived by someone

3. Disrespect toward you, a friend, or loved one

4. Being strongly devalued by someone

6. Violation of Trust

7. Abuse of Authority or Power

9. Being physically, verbally, financially, sexually, or emotionally abused, bullied or cheated

10. A friend, a loved one, a helpless person, or an innocent person being threatened, harmed, or abused

Chapter 15: Anger Differences

12. Being denied something that is very important to you

13. Someone wrongfully taking credit for your plan, idea, or achievement

15. Dishonoring or ignoring of requests, guidance, or instructions given to a subordinate or one's children, and the same neglect or opposition from one's spouse or coworker, when fulfillment of the requests, guidance, or instructions is appropriate

16. Passive or active "sabotage", delay, or blockage, by someone, of an idea, a solution, an objective, a task, a communication, or a project that is important to you

18. Anything (other than a person) that frustrates, hinders, or blocks something important to you

20. Someone identifying, pointing out, or telling you about your <u>true</u> faults, weaknesses, failings, wrong behaviors, etc.

The next six Core Emotional Issues are *moderately* likely to trigger anger reactions for men in general. Accordingly, that anger is most often moderate in strength.

5. Prejudice and Discrimination

8. Broken promises

11. Property Issues--your property being carelessly damaged or lost or being purposefully damaged or stolen

14. Personal failure in something that is very important to you

17. Anything that you consider to be meaningfully (to you) unjust or unfair

19. Abuse of your time

I have found that women in general in various world cultures, are more dominant in Giving Attributes (Chapter 4). Perhaps this is because of their many nurturing roles, their socialization to seek and build positive interpersonal relationships, their focus on interdependence, and their generally more civilized nature.

Women may get angry more from unfulfilled expectations, regarding the results of their giving, and from reaching a point of burn-out when they think that they are the only or main Givers in a relationship. On the other hand, men in general are probably more dominant in Balancing Attributes (Chapter 4). Perhaps this is because their major roles involve competition with others, a focus on independence, and in many cases, protecting the weak, helpless, and needy.

In western cultures, anger is more accepted when it is overtly expressed by males than when it is overtly expressed by females, although this does not mean that males are more angry in scope, frequency, or magnitude than females.

It is a fact that historically and currently, our world cultures operate in a continuous process of events, situations, and circumstances that appear in the short-term to be unfair. Because men have a higher need for justice in general, they often get angry easier about events, situations, and circumstances, which are or seem to be beyond their control.

Men's strong emotional need for justice and fairness in a seemingly and often real unjust and unfair world can lead to anger which in turn can lead to unhealthy overt actions including violence and abuse.

Age Anger Differences

Differing levels and combinations of maturity, frustration, control, and a sense of loss, are the elements of the age-related differences in anger. In general, a younger person gets angry easier regarding any limits to personal freedoms than does an older person. This is not simply an age issue, but also a maturity issue.

Most often, an older person has gained, learned, or programmed more correct thoughts and beliefs as the result of having experienced many more diverse life experiences as compared to most young persons. And so, the older person's expectations about human nature, relationships, situations, and events are generally more accurate and understood.

Conversely, a younger person often feels offended or unfairly treated in wider variety of life circumstances than does an older person. This is because of their having a major guiding belief that "life is unfair" or because of their limited understanding of how their complex society really functions. Younger people, who are less mature, most often have a strong belief in entitlement, that they are owed the good things of their culture without having to work for them or qualify for them.

There are some ages at which anger is more likely in general; these are the toddler years, adolescence, the 30s, and the 50s.

Anger is more likely during the toddler years, ages 2 to 4, because children at that age begin to realize that there are a lot of things that they want to do, but that they are not allowed to do. As they strive to be more independent, they are often frustrated by their own physical limitations and by the restrictions imposed on them by adults. They often become angry when their personal or selfish desires seem thwarted by caregiver rules and societal conventions such as learning to share, to be patient, and to be obedient to the requirements and instructions from adults, etc. They believe that they know best

Many of the same frustrations that exist during childhood also exist during adolescence. Teenagers believe that they know best, when in fact, they usually do not. About 70% of the adolescents, who are age 18 at any given time, are not yet able to do the mature formal operational

Chapter 15: Anger Differences

thinking that is very important for responsible adult living. Those adolescents who are beginning to gain this mature formal operational thinking, are still doing mostly concrete operational thinking and are only slowly transitioning into the more mature form of formal operational thinking.

One of the two fundamental problems with adolescent concrete operational thinking, is that while there is a fairly good understanding of freedom of choice and there is a reasonable competence in many areas of life, concrete operational thinkers exhibit a decided lack of understanding about the long term consequences of the choices that they make in the present. Immature adolescents live and act mostly only considering some of their present circumstances, without much if any rational consideration of future consequences, and without much restraint that is guided by things experienced through their past mistakes.

A second fundamental problem in immature adolescent thinking, is that it is mostly focused on the tangible things of their culture, without much consideration for or appreciation of the abstract matters that are the most important things in their culture, such as service, respect, meaningful learning, unselfishness, responsibility, etc.

Only approximately 30% of adolescents do a reasonable amount of formal operational thinking before age 19. Consequently, anger is quite likely to arise when restraints and limits are placed on the exercise of adolescents' perceived personal freedoms as they want to drive, date, seek employment, and explore the other major "adult" aspects of their culture, and develop plans for their future.

Anger in the 30s, when we are only just slightly past our peak physically and when we have often gained significant competence in our work or profession, is also related to the *false belief* that we know best about virtually everything (much like the child or adolescent). At that age, we often have little patience for the young and the old, because we are moving along in our life at a supposedly faster, more competent pace. We may also feel frustrated by the "old fashioned" ideas and goals of those who are in authority over us or who are perceived to be in the way of things that we want or that we want to achieve.

When we are in our 50s, anger issues are more likely to be related to some of the potential issues of a mid-life crisis. Those potential issues include, but are not limited to, being the sandwich generation with all of the burdens of taking care of parents and children, menopause, empty nest syndrome, noticeable sensory and physical decline, marital or intimate relationship unhappiness, fatigue, or having reached their work or professional limits/ceiling.

When we are in our 50s, often the perceived real loss of the "dream life" we imagined when younger may lead to anger against those we feel blocked our progress or inhibited our chances for success (including anger at self). Anger in the 50s may also be highly related to being unable to continue to advance in our work, careers, aspirations, or relationships. The *false belief* that life may be just about

Chapter 15: Anger Differences

enduring, or "downhill from here on out" can often lead to anger. Anger may also result from being devalued by those who are younger and who seem to have greater opportunities because of their age and energy.

Older adults, ages 60+, are more likely to get angry about the physical, work, and relationship losses that they typically experience as they age. These losses may include but are not limited to the loss of employment, loss of health, loss of sensory ability, loss of physical strength and mobility, loss of purpose, loss of respect and authority, and the loss of personal relationships through death, distance, or estrangement.

Socio-Economic Status (SES) Anger Differences

As for socio-economic status (SES) differences, there seems to be little or no differences in anger. However, a person who has more power due to financial resources, higher educational level, and higher social status is less likely to feel the effects of injustice simply because they are more able to influence the world around them for their personal benefit. Unfortunately, those at lower SES levels are more likely to be abused or offended by those in higher SES levels.

Additionally, no matter what our SES level is, we are likely to experience more frustration if we believe that many or most others around us, even if only seen on television or in movies, have more money, education, possessions, opportunities, and/or wealth than ourselves. This is known as relative deprivation. As it relates to SES, where desired resources are scarce and competition for those resources is strong, there is greater probability for Taking Behavior (Chapter 4), injustice, offense, abuse, and anger.

Ethnicity & Culture Anger Differences

Some ethnic or cultural groups have a very low tolerance for aggression and anger in their society (overtly and/or covertly), while other ethic or cultural groups encourage and even reward aggression and anger under the conditions approved/tolerated by their particular culture. Of course, the people of the world's numerous ethnic groups and cultures, in each group/culture, range across the whole spectrum of anger and aggression from virtually none to very much.

If you want to learn more about cultural ethnicity and it role in nurturing or inhibiting anger responses, you may want to do a good Google or library search to learn more about the Amish, Mennonites, Aboriginals, Thais, Maori, African Tribal Groups, Tongans, European Cultures, Mid-Eastern Cultures, Hispanic/Latino Cultures, and/or the various Asian Cultures.

Keep in mind that every ethnic or cultural group falls somewhere on the anger and aggression spectrum between low and high collective/average anger and aggression, and that there are a variety of both covert and overt ways that members of the many world ethnic or cultural groups express their anger and aggression.

Chapter 16

Ellen's Anger At Graduate School

6 Core Emotional Issues Violated and Their "Cost" to Ellen

There are potentially six Core Emotional Issues that might have been abused or violated in the following graduate school situation. Using what you have learned in previous Chapters, how many Core Emotional Issues can you identify?

This true anger story is about Ellen's anger experiences while she was attending graduate school. She attended graduate school full time for several years at a major university to earn a master's degree and then a doctorate degree in her chosen profession. Unfortunately, there were many opportunities for anger triggering and anger enhancing experiences.

Chapter 16: Ellen's Anger At Graduate School

Let me begin by telling you a bit about Ellen and her family. Ellen was an intelligent young woman, and, at age 28 when she entered graduate school, was older and more mature than the average graduate student. At that time, she had been married for eight years and was the mother of a beautiful little one year-old girl.

Ellen and her husband were very serious about being good parents so they mutually agreed that he would stay at home and that Ellen would go to school full time. They also agreed that because Ellen had greater earning ability, she would find and work at whatever work and assistantships that she could, to financially support their little family, and so that their daughter would have a consistent stay-at-home parent instead of having both parents gone much of the time.

Fortunately, Ellen was able to secure academic grants and assistantships as well as find sufficient part time or temporary employment opportunities to financially provide for her family. This allowed her husband to be an ideal father for their daughter and to be very supportive of Ellen considering her often hectic schedule.

This situation worked very well for their family for several years until just before the beginning of a new academic year. At that time, a powerful professor in Ellen's department realized that the only way for his favorite graduate student to compete successfully for the limited number of teaching assistantships was to eliminate Ellen from the competition. He did this by having Ellen placed on academic probation on the basis of her "not making

Chapter 16: Ellen's Anger At Graduate School

sufficient progress toward earning her graduate degrees".

The truth was though that Ellen actually had been making reasonable progress toward earning her desired graduate degrees. And, the faculty and graduate students involved knew that the academic probation was a wrong/immoral thing for the powerful professor to do, but he was too powerful for anyone to challenge him about it.

The loss of her teaching assistantship was emotionally devastating to Ellen because it represented half of her family's annual income. Consequently, she got very angry to the point of being enraged, because of the duplicity of the professor who had financially harmed her and her family. To make matters worse, Ellen learned that her major professor and mentor did not have the courage to challenge the offending professor. Fortunately, Ellen had sufficient maturity to keep her anger mostly to herself, rather than express it openly or let her anger motivate her to do something self defeating or unwise, considering her subordinate situation in her academic department.

Ellen's anger was very "costly" for her and her family because, for nine months, she could not effectively concentrate on anything else very well, other than the multiple injustices and harm that had been done to her and her family. That mental and emotional brooding turmoil that she experienced, over the wrongs that had been done to her, slowed her progress in finishing her graduate degrees and significantly interfered with the good quality of her family life. Her anger also harmed her physically due to the additional stress that it added to her already stressful life. That stress induced physical cost, also increased her susceptibility to allergies, illnesses, and abiding fatigue.

Unfortunately, this long lasting severe anger and rage episode was not the end of Ellen's graduate school problems and anger "costs". After Ellen had made arrangements for her doctoral research to be conducted at a very good research site near her campus, she was notified by the site administrators that a distant university had come to them after her arrangements were completed and approved, and had made arrangements with the site administrators such that only that distant university's graduate students were able to do research at Ellen's already approved site. Consequently, she was suddenly and unjustly denied access.

Ellen got angry about this duplicity, and because she was very determined to achieve justice, she tried to use the site anyway. Unfortunately, again Ellen's major professor did little to help her.

And so very soon, after trying her best to initiate her research at the nearby previously approved site, she was of course again thwarted and forbidden to proceed. She finally gave up her futile efforts, but she did not give up her anger.

In addition to anger, Ellen also developed a generous serving of depression about this situation. For several months, her angry and depressed emotional state was very costly to her and to her family. Finally, Ellen was mostly able to put her depression and anger behind her and continue

Chapter 16: Ellen's Anger At Graduate School

her graduate research at several other sites that she had to travel long distances to use. Seeking and finding a solution to her serious difficulty was very helpful, because it helped her to choose to feel more positive emotions and to achieve the progress in her academic work that was important to her.

Finally, after years of effort and many frustrations large and small, the day came for Ellen's oral doctoral defense of her research to a gathering of professors from her academic department. If you do not know about the seriousness of oral defenses, just know that this event can end with having wasted years of study and research if the assembled professors do not approve of what has been done.

An hour before her oral defense, Ellen met with her major professor for their last review of her doctorial dissertation document. In that meeting, he told her that she needed to change several things in the document before the oral defense.

Understand that by this time, Ellen had already made hundreds of changes which she and her major professor had discussed in their many meetings over the past several years. To say that she was "fed up" with making changes is a gross understatement of the negativity that she felt.

Ellen considered the new proposed changes to be trivial and unnecessary, especially at this, the last minute. Emboldened by her anger, she angrily asked her major professor if he thought she was going to be suddenly smarter after her oral defense ended with her being approved to be awarded a Ph.D. degree than she was right at this moment. It strongly triggered her anger to think that she was being treated as an "inferior" student prior to her review only to expect to be treated as a professional peer two hours later. She believed that this request by her major professor was a serious lack of respect for her hard earned academic and professional knowledge and abilities.

Because Ellen was emotionally "fed up", she got angry, said angry things to her mentoring major professor, and stormed angrily out of his office right before her oral defense was to commence. Her angry reactions and behavior threatened the success of years of struggle and hard work. Because Ellen's disrespectful behavior toward her major professor, he might have changed from a positive opinion about her being granted her Ph.D. degree to a negative opinion.

Fortunately for Ellen, her mentoring major professor was more emotionally mature than she was, and he retained his positive emotions and respect for Ellen and her academic achievements.

There were six Core Emotional Issues that were abused or violated in Ellen's graduate school experiences. Ellen's core emotion issues which provoked her disabling and wasteful anger and rage were:

Violation of trust: Ellen wrongfully trusted her major professor to protect and defend her appropriate academic interests and to always treat her as a mature adult.

Chapter 16: Ellen's Anger At Graduate School

Petty abuse of power: By the powerful professor in Ellen's academic department, by the research site, and by the distant university

Being financially abused: By the powerful professor in her academic department

Being denied something very important: Wrongful loss of her teaching assistantship which was very important for the financial support of her family

Important goal blocked: Her arranged and approved research site being pirated by a distant university

Being disrespected: Her belief that she was being treated as an inferior by her major professor at the end of her graduate studies experience

Ellen had a lot of *false expectations* that other people would respect her in the same way that she respected them, would treat her fairly as she treated them, and that in a professional educational setting, people would always make fair decisions. These false expectations about others were the most important problem for Ellen, and were the things that she ultimately could and did gain personal control of.

It would have been better for Ellen and for the others that she interacted with, during her graduate school years, if she had been more emotionally mature. In each case of her anger, she did not understand enough about the realities of life and about her own *false beliefs* and *false expectations* to circumvent the harmful emotional condition and harmful consequences of anger. Consequently, she needlessly experienced those things. But fortunately for her, Ellen suffered sufficiently to ultimately motivate her to want to develop greater understanding and maturity.

Ellen's anger, although seemingly justified, was not worth what it "cost" her and her family physically, mentally, socially, emotionally, and in time wasted!

Chapter 17

Hot Type A (Anger) Equals Premature Death

Physiological Destruction and Premature Death because of Anger

Over the past several decades, much has be learned and reported about individuals who are classified as having Type A personalities and about the attending thoughts, beliefs, emotions, and behaviors that are representative of that personality type. Just like all other personality types, that personality type, which is called a Type A personality, is composed of various characteristics or traits. And for any given individual who has a Type A personality, the characteristics or traits have differing strengths or amounts.

What most people do not realize though, is that some Type A personality individuals do not have the negative characteristics or traits that are harmful to them and others that they interact with, but do have the positive Type A characteristics or traits. These individuals, because of their absence of the negative traits, are known as **Cool Type A** personalities. And, those individuals who have an abundance of the negative and harmful characteristics or traits, in addition to having some or many of the productive ones, are known as **Hot Type A** personalities.

The single most destructive characteristic of a **Hot Type A** personality is <u>hidden hostility and anger</u>. And the second most destructive characteristic, is unrelenting time urgency, which creates and triggers frustration and anger.

It is thought that the basic cause of **Hot Type A** personality problems is insufficient valuing of self, or low self esteem. And so to repeat and emphasize, the two fundamental destructive characteristics of the **Hot Type A** personality are: (1) time urgency and impatience, which leads to frustration, irritation, and anger; and (2) unconscious free floating hostility, which expresses itself in anger and hostile behavior at the slightest provocation.

If you are interested in taking a free and informal Type A personality assessment, there are several online web-sites that will give you immediate scoring and feedback. I have listed the URLs for a few of these web-sites below. And if it so happens that the web-sites I have listed are no longer available when you read this, just do a Google search for free Type A Personality assessments and you will find other useful web-sites offering free assessments.

Chapter 17: Hot Type A Equals Premature Death

http://www.psych.uncc.edu/pagoolka/TypeAB.html

http://www.blogthings.com/doyouhaveatypeapersonalityquiz/

http://stress.about.com/library/Type_A_quiz/bl_Type_A_quiz.htm

    As a result of its anger related beliefs, thoughts, emotions, and behaviors, **Hot Type A** personality has been described as a risk factor for coronary disease by cardiologists Meyer Friedman and R. H. Rosenman. They estimated that **Hot Type A** behaviors by otherwise healthy individuals doubles the risk of coronary heart disease and an earlier death from that disease. In addition, according to research at Duke University by Redford Williams, the free floating hostility exhibited as anger, both hidden and expressed by **Hot Type A** personalities, is the only significant factor for causing their coronary heart disease and early death.

    As I mentioned before **Cool Type A** individuals do not have and do the anger related beliefs, thoughts, emotions, and behaviors, that **Hot Type A** personalities have and do, especially the hidden hostility and time urgency. **Cool Type A** behavior, thoughts, beliefs, and emotions are based on a selection of some or many the following characteristics and influences, which are intense but are also generally healthy. **Cool Type A** individuals may also have a few or small amounts of the negative **Hot Type A** characteristics, traits, or influences as well as the positive, productive, and healthy ones.

Positive Cool Type A Personality Characteristics, Traits, or Influences

- An intense and sustained drive to achieve goals
- An eagerness to compete
- Persistent desire for external recognition and advancement
- Engaging in many activities, without negative emotionality due to the completion and timing issues
- Accelerating mental and physical tasks with high alertness
- High achievement
- High power
- Often motivated by external things like material rewards and recognition

Hot Type A individuals' behaviors, beliefs, thoughts, and emotions are based on a selection of some or many of the following negative characteristics and influences.
Hot Type A individuals may also have or engage in some of the **Cool Type A** characteristics and influences.

Negative Hot Type A Characteristics, Traits, or Influences

- Often poorly defined and thus hard to achieve goals

Chapter 17: Hot Type A Equals Premature Death

- General discontentedness
- Impulses to be highly critical and inappropriately demanding of others
- Contempt about imperfection in self and others' work or achievements
- Bursts of anger and other forms of overt and covert hostility
- Impatience with self and others
- Guilt, remorse, and fear
- Feelings of being constantly opposed by others or circumstances
- Constant wariness and apprehension
- Constant readiness for engaging in conflict
- Unhappy
- Rigidity
- High job, relationships, and family stress
- Low valuing of self or low self esteem
- Social isolation caused by alienating others and not investing in positive friendships
- Facial tension like wrinkled brow, pursed lips, clenched jaw, etc.
- Teeth grinding, dark circles under the eyes, forehead and upper lip sweating
- Hypertension and high blood pressure
- Much higher risk for coronary disease and early death

Based on the above list, I hope that it is easy to tell that the negative **Hot Type A** personality traits are destructive, antisocial, and generally, self-defeating.

In this chapter, have presented some of the information about Type A Personality in a true but condensed form. It is good to remember that each of us has a personality with hundreds of traits and that each of those personality traits vary in complexity, strength, amount, and in the ways that they influence our individual lives.

Almost all individuals with Cool Type A Personalities also have some the negative traits as well. And the strength or amount of the negative and positive things varies from low to high for any of them that they have or experience.

Almost all individuals with Hot Type A Personalities (especially the worst two traits) also have some the positive traits as well. And the strength or amount of the positive and negative things varies from low to high for any of them that they have or experience.

If one is a Type A person, it is a very good idea to identify, reduce, and eliminate his or her negative Hot Type A personality traits, because those things weaken and destroy our bodies as well as generate a lot of personal and interpersonal unhappiness.

Chapter 18

Roger's Anger Over The Years

High Need for Control and Anger from Frustrations Resulting From Control Issues

The main Core Emotional Issues involved in the following episodes from Roger's life involve things that frustrated, hindered, or blocked something important to him. Roger also had Core Emotional Issues involving a high personal need for control. And as if that was not difficult enough, he was also very sensitive about petty abuse of power by others toward him.

During my years of counseling others to help them have greater success and happiness, I have discovered that many of us have a high need for control but also a low understanding of what we can effectively control or what is appropriate to try to control. This combination of high need and low understanding, naturally results in a lot of frustration, unhappiness, and anger. Such was the case for Roger. To illustrate how control issues are powerful stimulants/triggers of anger and anger's various resulting problems, I will share 4 control stories from Roger's life.

The first story only involved a moderate amount of control frustration for Roger and thus only a moderate amount of unhappiness for him. It had to do with his wife's sewing machine. It was a quality sewing machine with a guarantee which promised free replacement parts, if and when needed due to normal wear. As it so happened after nine years, a part broke. So Roger, guarantee in hand, went to the nearest sewing machine dealer to get the part so that he could fix the machine himself in order to save the cost of having someone else repair it.

When Roger asked for the free part, the dealer told him that he could only get the free part if the dealer installed it. Of course, the installation came with a hefty repair fee. That annoyed and frustrated Roger, but he decided to control his negative emotions and behaviors in hopes of getting the part that he wanted without having to pay for the repair.

So, Roger showed the dealer the guarantee which said nothing about the part having to be installed by the dealer. The dealer told Roger again that he could not have the part without installation by the dealer. This frustrated Roger a lot. He got very angry, and then said some unkind things to the sewing machine dealer.

Chapter 18: Roger's Anger Over The Years

Although he felt justified, Roger's getting angry and expressing it did not help the situation, and probably only made the dealer more resolved to get paid for the repair. Additionally, Roger wasted a lot of his personal time dealing with his angry thoughts and feelings.

Several days later, Roger resolved to write the sewing machine company and ask for the part directly from them. In his letter, he mentioned the "rude and unfair" treatment that he felt he received from the dealer. After some delay, the company representative replied, and to Roger's dismay, the company also refused to give him the part without having the machine repaired by the local dealer.

As a result, Roger got even angrier. He stewed and stewed over the "wrong and offensive treatment" that he felt he was consistently getting from the company and its local dealer. And so finally, he resorted to initiating legal action against them. That did the trick. The company sent the part to Roger. Hooray, Roger won!! It is worth getting angry when your core emotional issues are violated.

Or was it? The local repair service would have cost $80. Roger spent about five days worth of time thinking about the offense he felt he had wrongfully endured instead of using his time productively. At this time in his life, he was making about $100 a day so his anger cost him about $500 instead of $80. Also, Roger was unhappy on and off for two months during this episode. What is the value of his lost happiness, contentment and peace of mind? This is not to mention, that the quality of life for Roger's wife was also reduced during this time, because while Roger's anger was not aimed at his wife, it hurt her nonetheless.

A few years later, Roger and his wife were driving on a very busy interstate highway to visit Roger's mother. As often happens on busy highways, another driver in the passing lane was driving dangerously close behind Roger, even though Roger was driving slightly over the speed limit. This was frustrating and annoying to Roger, because he felt that the other driver was needlessly endangering him and his wife.

Sadly, Roger was not mature enough to quickly move over so that the driver could pass him. Instead, he slowed down and then sped up to "teach" the dangerous driver behind him to follow at a safer distance. This caused the driver behind him to be more determined to follow dangerously close to Roger, all the while flashing his lights.

At that point, Roger got really angry and waved with his hand for the other driver to back off. The other driver did not. In his anger, Roger decided to slow down to match the speed of the traffic in the slower lane and then slowed down even more. This enraged the other driver, and he followed even closer. As that was happening, Roger was getting more and more angry.

Finally after much fear and pleading by Roger's wife and much frustration and anger on Roger's part, Roger sped up and moved to the slower lane when it was safe to do so. The tailgating driver sped angrily by and no doubt had his

Chapter 18: Roger's Anger Over The Years

day ruined with his ongoing angry thoughts, emotions, and behaviors. The tailgating driver may well have spread his unhappiness to others as he went through the rest of his day as is often the case when we get angry. Fortunately for everyone, the other driver did not shoot Roger or try to harm him in some other way.

While it is true that the other driver was immature and did indeed endanger Roger and his wife, Roger's resulting anger, fear, and dangerous actions did not make the situation better and actually made several things worse. Much of the potential happiness of that day was spoiled for Roger, for his wife, and probably for several other people that they interacted with during their visit. Although he did not realize it Roger also lost some degree of his wife's trust, because in his anger, he too had endangered her safety. And, Roger, because of his choices in this situation, strengthened his anger habit and therefore increased negative effects from this anger habit going forward in his life.

Nothing was learned or truly gained by anyone from Roger's anger and dangerous behavior in this situation.

Anger does not really fix things. However, it does leave large emotional messes in its wake. The set of anger habits that Roger built and strengthened for himself had long lasting negative effects on his life and the lives of others that he influenced or associated with.

So sadly, for many years after this anger on the highway event, Roger often still automatically reacted with strong and enduring frustration and anger when he felt violated, harmed, and frustrated by others while driving.

There are many bureaucratic organizations that one has to deal with from time to time, and in those organizations, there are employees who have power to help or hinder us in our dealings with them. Sometimes, those employees wrongfully abuse their power to try to avoid making decisions, to control us, or to teach us that we are less important than them or are subservient to them. This next real life experience involves Roger at a post office.

In this experience, Roger was moving away from a temporary work location, and he was instructed by his company that they had an arrangement with the post office to allow Roger to mail many of his work files and belongings at no cost to him. This financial advantage was nice for Roger, because he was not paid very much at his job.

Two days before he was to move, Roger carried 10 large, heavy boxes of files and personal possessions to the local post office with his company's official mailing permission documents. Since Roger did not have a car at the work location, and the post office was three blocks from his apartment, he had to carry the heavy boxes to the post office himself.

When Roger got to the post office counter, he explained what his company had told him about mailing, and he showed the postal clerk the company's mailing permission documents. To Roger's dismay, the postal clerk

Chapter 18: Roger's Anger Over The Years

refused to honor the documents and told Roger that he would have to pay approximately $400 for mailing the boxes.

Roger was frustrated by this "obviously wrong and unfair" treatment, and he quickly got very angry. Fortunately, by this time in his life, he had learned not to say mean or abusive things to people who were frustrating his goals, but he did angrily demand to talk with a supervisor, and he did angrily demand that the free mailing agreement be honored. At that, the postal clerk refused again and left the counter to go into the back room of the post office to avoid having to deal with Roger any more.

Roger reacted to this service abandonment and insult with extreme frustration and anger. He could hardly see clearly because of his extreme anger, so he left his boxes on the post office floor and went outside to compose himself. After about 15 minutes, he angrily went back in the post office, carried his boxes outside, and stacked them on a bench in the front of a store next to the post office. Having no car, Roger had to hand-carry the heavy boxes one by one back to his apartment. When there, Roger called his supervisor and asked her to intervene with the post office manager.

After Roger had carried two of the ten boxes back the three blocks to his apartment, he received a call from the police asking if he was the owner of the boxes in front of the store. He told them that he was, and they told him to come to the store right away. When he got to the store by the post office, the police officer asked him who he was, if the boxes were his, and told him that he had to remove the boxes immediately.

Roger showed his photo ID to the police officer to identify himself, and explained his situation. He then asked why he had to hurry more to move his boxes, when he was already doing the best he could. The police officer told him that someone had reported that the boxes were a potential bomb threat. Roger explained that he was mailing the boxes, which were clearly labeled with his present and future addresses, and asked who had reported the threat. The officer told him he did not know, but the boxes had to be moved immediately.

With obvious frustration and anger, Roger took the rest of the heavy boxes one by one back to his apartment, while the police officer stood by the remaining boxes and watched for compliance.

After a few trips back and forth to return the boxes to his apartment, Roger again asked the police officer who had called in the bomb threat, and then the officer told Roger that it had been the postal clerk who called in this obviously false bomb threat.

Upon learning about the source of this additional "abuse", Roger's anger ramped up again, but fortunately he did not say anything negative to the police officer. After carrying all of the boxes back to his apartment, Roger got a call from his supervisor telling him to forget about the clerk,

Chapter 18: Roger's Anger Over The Years

and that in this case, the company would pay up front for the mailing. It seemed to Roger that his supervisor did not care that Roger had been wronged, and only wanted the problem to be resolved as quickly as possible. Her apparent attitude about the abuse Roger was experiencing added to Roger's already massive anger, but fortunately he was mature enough to keep quiet and thus keep his job.

It is true that Roger was treated badly, unfairly, and even abusively. However, Roger was the one who had to "pay" the most for the problems, because he was frustrated and angry for weeks afterwards. He had gained an enemy in the person of the postal clerk, in addition to losing respect from and for his work supervisor.

It would have been better for Roger and everyone he interacted with in this matter, if he had been more emotionally mature. He then would have understood the lack of maturity of the postal clerk and would have found a much more positive way to achieve his goals. He also would have emotionally accepted that at times, things that are important to him are not always important to others, and that things do not always go smoothly, as hoped for, or as planned.

With greater emotional maturity, Roger would have changed his beliefs, thinking, feelings and behaviors from destructive ones to productive ones. Anger is not worth the "cost" to the ones who get angry nor to the ones who are harmed by the negative effects of that anger.

Chapter 18: Roger's Anger Over The Years

My final account of Roger's frustration and anger involves his family. Roger and his wife wanted to have children, but they did have their first baby until six years after they were married. Their firstborn was a lovely girl. Roger and his wife were thrilled to finally be parents, even though they, like many other parents, had a lot to learn about parenting. At first, all went well with their changed family structure. But before long, a serious problem began to develop between Roger and his wife because of the addition of their daughter to their family relationships.

Roger's wife was an attentive and loving person, but because she had waited so long for her first baby, and because being a good mother was very important to her, she was focusing almost all of her attention and love on her daughter and very little on Roger.

At first, Roger did not mind this absence of love and attention from his wife, because he thought this behavior was typical for all new mothers. However, he eventually became very frustrated by this situation when his feelings of neglect and loneliness continued for months. As time went on, from months to years without any meaningful change in this pattern, Roger's resentment and hidden anger steadily increased. Unfortunately, most of the time, Roger was not consciously aware of the negative emotionality that was gradually accumulating in him.

The spousal inattention conditions in Roger's marriage did not improve with the arrival of their second daughter. His feelings of being neglected continued, and the

Chapter 18: Roger's Anger Over The Years

marriage relationship was increasingly unhappy, because unfortunately in addition to the relationship neglect Roger experienced, he also found that his wife frequently devalued and frustrated his parenting behaviors and plans.

It seemed to Roger that nothing he could do or say helped put the spousal relationship back in its proper, uppermost place in the family hierarchy and that his parenting efforts were increasingly being devalued by his wife. This situation was immensely frustrating, and it stimulated a deep and abiding, but hidden anger in Roger. He felt severely devalued and additionally was often very discouraged about these matters.

For Roger, one of the most infuriating manifestations of being devalued as a parent by his wife, was her continued interference in his child discipline efforts. Despite her promise to never interfere with his disciplining of their daughters, she often sided with their daughters against his discipline, by interfering with or changing what he was doing to correct their daughters.

To be fair to Roger's wife, it was probably easier and more rewarding for her to build her relationships with their two daughters than to do so by working with "strongly opinionated and emotionally sensitive" Roger. And most likely, it was also easy for her to believe that her ways of parenting were better than his ways.

As best that I learned, in most ways, Roger's wife was a more skilled and knowledgeable parent than Roger was. Consequently, she did not trust or value many of his parenting efforts. This, coupled with her commitment to be a good mother, made it very easy for her to favor her daughters and to disfavor and neglect Roger, most likely without realizing the harm it was doing to him and to their marital relationship.

The way his wife devalued and neglected Roger was to him, clearly wrong and deeply hurtful to him. And Roger's imperfections and weaknesses in his role as a husband and a father were also damaging and self defeating for him. Roger's and his wife's combined imperfections resulted in years of unhappiness for them both and a lot of incorrect spousal and parenting examples for their children.

Roger's and his wife's long term resentment and anger toward each other in relation to these matters, may have been justified, but the anger did not resolve anything.

The good news for Roger and his wife according to my last report, is that after their children were adults, he and his wife finally began consistently working on improving their spousal relationship and subsequently are much happier.

It was *false beliefs* and *false expectations* that Roger and his wife had formed about each other that were the root or core of Roger's and his wife's spousal problems.

Instead of striving to control each other, instead of devaluing each other, instead of opposing each other, all of which resulted in emotional pain, frustration, and anger, it was forgiveness, effective communication, trust, kindness, and personal commitment to self-improvement by Roger and his wife that greatly improved Roger's and his wife's relationship with each other into a more happy and successful one.

Chapter 19

Why Anger Is Not Necessary

The Short Version

Over the past few years whenever I have had the opportunity to teach groups of individuals about eliminating anger, almost always someone speaks up for his or her belief in the need to keep the anger. This objection to the complete elimination of anger is quite common and almost universal. Taken at its face value, this objection seems very reasonable. However, over the years of my scientific/professional life, I have never been able to find a good reason to keep personal anger vs. other methods to achieve our good purposes.

When this objection to the elimination of anger arises, I always ask for *specific* good reasons for keeping anger.

Chapter 19: Why Anger Is Not Necessary

In the following parenthesis, I will list all of the good reasons provided by others.

(   )

There are <u>not</u> any good reasons!

Anger harms, disables, and even handicaps us mentally, socially, physically, emotionally, and spiritually. It is a major waste of our positive constructive and developmental time. Where is the good in that?

I do believe that we need to individually experience anger so as to understand how it feels, and to come to understand that it leads to a multitude of unhappy consequences. I also have found that it is important for us to have personal experiences with anger and its elimination so that we can understand how to help each other get rid of it.

When you are ready to eliminate your anger habits, there is a way. It works. While the anger elimination method is simple to understand, it is often harder to emotionally accept the changes that are required than you would suppose. In any case learn for yourself in the next chapter, My Most Important Insight About Anger Elimination (Chapter 20).

Chapter 20

My Most Important Insight About Anger Elimination

You can and will eliminate your anger towards anyone, if you choose to change in the necessary ways.

As I told you in a previous chapter, in 2005, I sincerely promised my wife that I would <u>NEVER</u> be angry with her again!

By this I meant I would not get angry at all or if I slipped and got angry, I would correct that privately and in a few minutes at the most.

You are most likely saying to yourself, "This promise is crazy! I thought this guy was a psychologist. Everybody knows that you get angry sometimes, no matter what your best intentions are or what you would rather do."

Chapter 20: My Most Important Insight

My promise was not made rashly, or even in a moment of insanity, nor was it a foolish or immature promise. I was able to make that promise and keep it in the way that I have described because I finally understood what was wrong in my own beliefs. It was my false beliefs about myself and others that were causing my anger across my life. While my insight was certainly personal, it also applies to you and anyone else.

So, This Is The Insight

"What a person is doing or not doing, believing or not believing, thinking or not thinking, feeling or not feeling, choosing or not choosing at any given time **is the evidence** of the best that they can do at that time, given (1) their current maturity level, (2) the effects of their near term and long term life situations, and (3) any of the external environmental influences, as those things in any way affect him or her in any way."

Think about it this way, what a person is doing at any given time is the best that he or she can do at that time, otherwise they would be doing it better. Think about the last mistake that you made and ask yourself, "Why did I not do better?" The plain and simple reason was that, at that current maturity level at that point in your life, and considering the physical, environmental, social, emotional, spiritual, and mental circumstances that were influencing you at that time in your life, you were doing the best that you could at that moment.

The best evidence of what a person can do in any area of his or her life is what he or she did do, did not do, is doing, or is not doing. This applies equally to a person's thoughts, beliefs, emotions, and behaviors done or not done.

The reason that we or others think that we or they can do or should have done "better" about something that is or was important to us or them, is that all of us have the ability to conceive of something that is better than our current level of maturity in that thing. If we could not do that, we would never be able to improve in our thinking, beliefs, attitudes, emotions, and/or behaviors.

Being able to understand what is better in thoughts, beliefs, attitudes, emotions, and/or behaviors, does not mean that we are mature enough to change to being able to do better at that time. It is our *false beliefs* about ourselves, in terms of understanding of our current developmental level, that results in us getting angry about our own "failures" to do what we think we should be able to do, but in fact cannot do.

It is our *false expectations* about others' thoughts, beliefs, emotions, understandings, and behaviors that cause us to get angry at them about what they do and don't do in those things. We believe that they can and should think better, believe better, feel better, understand better, do better in current situations and could have and should have done better in any of these ways in past situations.

Chapter 20: My Most Important Insight 149

These are *false expectations* because what the "guilty" person did or did not do is the only credible evidence of the best that they could or could not do at the time. Likewise, what the "guilty" person is or is not doing in his or her behaviors is the only credible evidence of the best that he or she can currently do or not do in his or her behaviors. As I said before, we also generate *false expectations* about the "guilty" person's past and current thinking, beliefs, understandings, attitudes, and feelings which are done and not done.

However, this does not mean that they cannot or should not improve! Changing our expectations based on the **evidence on hand** does not mean that we approve of or permanently accept wrong behavior, thinking, beliefs, understanding, attitudes, and emotions. It just means that we mentally and especially **totally emotionally accept** the current developmental state and environmental influences that is the reality for the person involved.

One reason why we think that others can do better when they disappoint, offend, or abuse us is that we might have observed them doing better with someone else or at some other time. The reason that they did better previously was because conditions were more favorable for them at that time or with that person. All of us have a range of how well we do about any given thing or with any given person.

When our life situation, our relationships' conditions, our mood, our frame of mind, our fatigue, our hunger, our wellness, or any other influence is good or stable, we do better in any of our categories or domains of thinking, beliefs, understandings, attitudes, feelings, and behaviors.

Conversely, when our life situation, our relationships' conditions, our mood, our frame of mind, our fatigue, our hunger, our wellness, or any other influence is more negative or deficient, we perform worse than our best in any of our categories or domains of thinking, beliefs, understandings, attitudes, feelings, and behaviors.

Assuming that anger elimination is your goal, there are a few simple concepts that you need to **understand and then honestly and emotionally fully commit to embracing and living** in order for you to totally eliminate your anger from your life. Those concepts are as follows:

First: We frequently make mistakes in our relationships with and treatment of others because of our *false belief* that people have a maturity level that matches their chronological age. Additionally, we naturally and unconsciously usually believe that others should be at least as mature about any given thing as we are. This is also a *false belief* and a mistake.

The truth is that each of us is at different levels of maturity for each of our hundreds of personal traits, habits and skills like kindness, patience, creativity, thoughtfulness, conscientiousness, sociality, courage, sensitivity, trust, intimacy, self-sufficiency, personal discipline, spirituality, physical fitness, self valuation, altruism, discernment, tolerance, helpfulness, parenting, memory, responsibility,

Chapter 20: My Most Important Insight

communication, listening, self-awareness, valuing others, forgiving, gratitude, etc.

Second: There is no obligation for any of us to be at the same maturity level as others in one or any of our traits. Of course it is convenient and very helpful when it works out that way. Unfortunately, the odds are that we are at a different maturity level for any given trait, than are others that we interact with, whether they are strangers or even are people that we know well. It is a *false belief* to believe otherwise.

Third: All of us human beings are able to form habits in our thinking, beliefs, emotions, and behaviors. When a habit about anything is formed, we do not have to consciously decide exactly how to think, believe, feel, or behave. We react automatically. We use anger this way.

The good news is that we can change any thinking, belief, emotional, or behavioral habit that we want to change. This means that you can totally eliminate your anger habits just as I have done and am doing. I have explained how to replace any and all negative habits in Reducing Anger by Replacing Your Anger Habits (Chapter 7).

Fourth: Being angry is destructive to you and others. Our anger drains us of valuable energy. It squanders our assets of time and happiness. It robs us of productivity and peace of mind. See Chapters 1, 3, 11, 14, and 16 for more about this topic.

Fifth: We as human beings need to experience anger to understand it. However, once we experience and understand anger, it is not necessary for us to continue to use it or wallow in it. That is, anything good that may be associated with anger or result because of it, can be achieved without anger. Being forgiving and calm instead of angry allows us to solve our problems much quicker and more effectively. We can be and need to be in a high state of mental and physiological arousal from time to time, but anger only dilutes or weakens our effectiveness in those situations. We can activate and maintain that positive and effective aroused state without being angry in any way.

Sixth: For you to change/eliminate your anger habits, you must remain consciously aware of what you are thinking and believing about people and situations. When we are consciously aware, we can choose the *true* thoughts, beliefs, emotions and behaviors that eliminate anger. Those true thoughts, beliefs, emotions and behaviors naturally replace the false ones. As we consciously choose this positive replacement happens gradually over time and becomes our automatic positive reactions to difficult or challenging things. Meaningful positive human change or development is a process not an event. Refer to the process of forming new habits outlined in Reducing Anger by Replacing Your Anger Habits (Chapter 7).

Seventh: In addition to fully understanding the above concepts, **true and complete emotional commitment to personally live them is necessary** for you to eliminate anger from your life.

Chapter 20: My Most Important Insight

At this point let me suggest that you will have the greatest and quickest success in eliminating your anger when you:

***Choose to emotionally* trust** that injustice will be fully rectified and that justice will be accomplished in the long term on its own without your need to correct it in the near term.

Allow your insight (True Intuition) to assure you that you do not have to correct injustice and offenses.

Stay Consciously Aware of and ***Choose to Correct*** your false thoughts, beliefs, understandings, attitudes, emotions, and behaviors about situations, people, etc.

Accept mentally and emotionally, that each of us is doing the best that we can do at any given time, considering our individual maturity levels and the positive or negative circumstances that alter whether we are acting at the top, middle, or bottom of our range of competence.

Eliminating anger can and will increase your productivity and improve your relationships. Letting go of your anger can and will enrich your life, will provide a foundation for inspiration and peace, and will enhance your physical, mental and emotional sense of well being. It can and will reduce stress, anxiety and the accompanying physical symptoms of high blood pressure, coronary disease, and even early death.

Honestly and diligently applying the true principles in this book can and will take you from the Anger Path to the path of greater happiness, inner peace and contentment, and life success.

If you have been helped by what I have written and you want to help your associates, friends, and loved ones reduce and eliminate their anger, then I invite you to share with them what you have learned and how you have applied the insights in this book.

If you would like further information or help about eliminating your anger, you can presently contact me at:

angerelimination@gmail.com.

Appendix A
Additional Anger Stories & The Core Emotional Issues Involved

The following true stories that have been given to me, are in the words of the people who experienced them, and have only a few edits on my part for confidentiality and clarity.

Sam's Anger: His Friend's Selfishness

Susan's Anger: Trust Violation, Disrespect, Property Damage

Maria's Anger: Being Lied to, Being Financially Abused

Sahar's Anger: Classmate Being Bullied

Jose's Anger: Lies & "Sabotage"

Ranesia's Anger: Trust Violation, Harm to Family

Zixin's Anger: Emotional Abuse

Ahmed's Anger: Disrespect, Trust Violation, Property Harm

Isaac's Anger: Emotional, Physical, and Property Abuse

Isabella's Anger: Disrespect, Time Abuse, Wrongful Credit

Travon's Anger: Violation of Trust, Loved One Harmed

Daniel's Anger: Theft, Lies, Trust Violation

Sam's Anger: His Friend's Selfishness

Core Emotional Issues

- 6 (Violation of Trust)
- 16 (Passive or active "sabotage", delay, or blockage, by someone, of an idea, a solution, an objective, a task, a communication, or a project that is important to you)
- 17 (Anything that you consider to be meaningfully unjust or unfair)

Around last fall when we first moved into our new three-bedroom apartment, an issue about who would get which bedroom arose. The three bedrooms unfortunately were uneven sizes, with one room being especially small. So to be fair about it all, we decided to alter rent payments to match the corresponding room sizes. Still, no one jumped to take the small room because all of us knew that we would have trouble storing our furniture.

During the duration of this "who gets the small room" issue, my roommate Jeremy and I found that the third roommate Roger, to be unjust and unfair, as well as unreasonable. Previous to our conflict with Roger, I felt ready to accept the small room knowing that Jeremy had just previously moved out of a fully furnished studio apartment. Therefore he had the most things to fit into a room. So I assumed that it would be best for him to have one of the larger bedrooms. It is also to be noted that both Jeremy and I had no place to store our things because our parents had no storage room for our things because for my parents, other furniture was bought after I moved out of the house, and Jeremy's parents moved to a smaller house after his graduation from high school.

The three of us decided that each of us one at a time should try moving all of his individual things into the small room and then decide who could best fit his things in the room on a permanent basis after that. I started trying to fit my things into the small bedroom first, by moving my queen bed into the room and trying two different setups. I explained to my roommates that if needed I could switch beds at my parents' house to a smaller one to make it work. And I said I probably could possibly store all of my art projects and supplies in the small closet space.

Next, Jeremy tried fitting all of his things into the room. Soon, he realized he could not fit his bookshelf in that room, so he decided that if it came down to it, he would throw away his bookshelf to make his remaining things fit. Roger was next and the atmosphere completely changed from "willing to make things work" to "selfish notions."

Roger then began fitting his things into the small bedroom. He started by putting his large oak dresser into the small closet because he said that he "needs" it for his clothes. Jeremy and I both asked him if it would be all right if he were to ditch the dresser and just hang his clothes on the rack provided in the closet. This was an instant problem because he "always kept his clothes in a dresser". We asked, "Could you change that to make it work for the room?" He replied with a defiant "No."

After the issue of the poor use of closet space, next came the issue of the bed in the wrong place. When we helped Roger move his furniture into the small bedroom, we arranged his furniture in a way that gave him the most square footage of open space to walk around in. Suddenly, a new problem arose: The bed was oriented such that Roger's head would be by the door when he was sleeping in his bed, and he told us that he did not like sleeping in that fashion. Again, we asked if he could give up that small preference to accommodate the ideal arrangement of his furniture in the small room. We were met with the same answer as before, a defiant "no".

At that point I notice that I had gotten pretty angry. Mostly, from Roger's unjust reasons to keep being selfish when both Jeremy and I were ready to give up things to make things work if need be. For me, this situation of noncooperation and negativity by Roger had changed my feelings from happy cooperation to one of the most frustrating and angry times in my life. It felt like I was working with a spoiled little child.

My anger lasted as long as the situation did, and the situation lasted for quite a long time from my perspective. Once each of us had tried to fit his thing in the small bedroom, the clear and best decision about who should take that room, was for Roger to take the small bedroom. But that reasonable decision was apparently too big of a hit to

Roger's spoiled ego and obviously he couldn't take it. Jeremy and I tried and tried to convince Roger that our perspective was correct and reasonable, but he would not be convinced. Instead he only increased in his resistance to being assigned to the small bedroom.

In the end, Jeremy and I were exhausted from trying to convince Roger that it would work the best for everyone for him to be in the small bedroom, so I ended up taking the small bedroom myself. During the situation I wanted very much to yell at Roger about his selfishness. I believe that at the time, yelling angrily at Roger would have changed his mind out of his fear of me.

Instead of angry yelling, what ended up actually happening, is both Jeremy and I tried to stay calm and explain things logically to Roger. And as I stated before, that had absolutely zero effect on getting Roger to do the right thing.

After taking the small room, I found that my living space in that small bedroom was too small to be able to be lived in comfortably, so I spend most of my time in the living room, only leaving my bedroom for what it was so aptly named: a bed room. After a week or two, I finally let go of most of my inner frustration and anger. And then I finally began to appreciate the advantage of the cheaper rent.

Susan's Anger about Trust, Disrespect, and Property Damage

Core Emotional Issues

- 3. Disrespect toward you, a friend, or loved one
- 6. Violation of Trust
- 9. Being physically, verbally, financially, sexually, or emotionally abused, bullied or cheated
- 11. Your property being carelessly or purposefully lost, damaged, or stolen

My anger can best be described as high levels of frustration. There are many feelings twisting and turning through the body. I notice when I am angry an increase in adrenaline, heart rate begins to beat harder, and a million things going through my mind. I recently had my anger flair up and I remember all the feelings and emotions going on.

A couple days ago my roommate and I were sitting on our futon watching Jersey Shore. I was starting to get tired and was thinking about going to sleep but Emily, my roommate, was wide awake. She then proceeded to ask me if some boys could come over that were her friends. I wasn't too thrilled with the idea but I told her they could come over. The boys that come over are the kind of boys who are spoiled brats. They never care about consequences or think about the outcome of things. A little while later, Emily leaves the room and lets the boys in through the security door.

While I am sitting in my room I can hear the boys being obnoxious in the hallway and I knew something interesting would happen that night. I look at the door and everyone comes bursting into the room. One of the boys walks straight to the futon and the other to my computer desk. I chose to sit on the ottoman to make sure I could watch everyone. I glance over to Paul, the one at the desk, and notice him with scissors cutting my lanyard in half. I did not understand why he would do that and became slightly upset. I was just happy that I just purchased a new lanyard a couple days before. I soon forced myself to forget about that tiny problem.

All of us began talking and were starting to have a good time. I glance at Paul again and he is cutting my box of Kudos bars and completely destroying the box. This incident did not bother me at all because it was just a box that I really did not need any more. We all began talking again for awhile and next thing we know we hear Paul chime up and say, "What does this go to?" I look at him and he is swinging in the air a piece of my computer adapter. I do not understand how he could cut my computer cord so now I could not charge my computer. Instantly, my body tensed up, heart beat increased, thoughts swimming through my mind, and loads of adrenaline pumping through my body.

I stand up and begin screaming, "Get out of my room NOW!" I said this over and over. All he did was just stare at me and say, "I did not do it." Everyone in the room knew that was a lie. All I could think about was that I needed my computer to write this paper. My emotions were running wild. I noticed no one was leaving my dorm room and I decided I will leave my room if no one else will. I took off and went outside. I started walking around to calm myself down. I was thinking about a lot of things at the time. I considered going to his room and cutting his computer cord but I knew that was not nice at all in the first place.

After walking around for forty-five minutes, I was calmer and thinking clearly. But every time I thought of what Paul did I would just become furious. I was upset that he lied to me and did not say sorry it was a mistake and I will buy you a new one. He did not care about the situation at all.

I ventured back to the dorms and my room with a mind that was thinking crystal clear. Walking around has always helped me to calm down and I knew if I went straight to bed things would be better in the morning. I made a plan with Paul that I would purchase a new one and he would pay me back. I was extremely lucky that Wal-Mart sold HP power adapters and that I would not have to order one online.

One of the core emotional issues fits my angry experience perfectly. My property was carelessly or purposefully lost, damaged, or stolen. For some reason my property is always ruined by other people. I do not understand why. I do trust people using or borrowing my things. If you are a good friend I will not even worry about you doing anything wrong to my things. But if you are someone I don't really know well, I am less likely going to let you use my things.

Appendix A: Additional Anger Stories

If your friends borrow your things and they break it you know they will do the right thing and either fix it or purchase you a new one. I soon found out that Paul must not be that great of friend to me because at first he was not going to buy me a new one. The issue to Paul was not a big deal. My thoughts on this were completely opposite.

My view on anger is it is an emotion dealing with high levels of frustration. Anger issues can be interesting. It is fascinating to find out how people deal with their anger because everyone does it differently. Sometimes it takes a lot for people to become angered and others a little flick to the ear can have them blow up. Everyone has their own ideas and thoughts about anger.

Maria's Anger about Being Lied to and Being Financially Abused

Core Emotional Issues

- 2. Being used, tricked, lied to, or deceived by someone
- 6. Violation of Trust
- 9. Being physically, verbally, financially, sexually, or emotionally abused, bullied or cheated

This past summer I worked for the public pools in the town where I live. It was an awesome job that I really enjoyed. While I enjoyed my job for the most part and got alone with most of the people I worked with there were downsides to the job. The hours were long, often up to fifty-five a week and a lot was expected of me. One thing that made the long hours worthwhile was knowing at the end of the summer a two hundred dollar bonus was coming my way.

During my last week at work one of my bosses came in and told Me and my co-workers that we wouldn't be getting the bonus. Instantly anger started rising up inside me. I didn't say anything because other people were asking most of the questions that I had in mind. How could they lie to us all summer about the bonus? Why weren't we getting it? Whose decision was it to not give us the bonus? Looking back I'm glad I didn't say anything because it probably wouldn't have been well thought out and I most likely would have regretted it.

The main thing that was the cause of my anger is that I felt I had been betrayed. I had worked long hours all summer long for these people and they had been lying to me. The reason they said we were no longer getting our bonuses was because of a miss print in the contracts we signed. I didn't understand why they couldn't just change the miss print in the contracts so they we could still get our bonuses.

Looking back on the experience I realize that I had a legitimate reason to be angry. To resolve my anger it helped talking to co-workers. Knowing that I wasn't alone in the situation helped me feel better about it. Also knowing that any other summer job I would have gotten most likely would not have offered me a bonus either.

Sahar's Anger: Classmate Bullied

Core Emotional Issues

- 5. Prejudice and Discrimination
- 10. A friend, a loved one, a helpless person, or an innocent person being threatened, harmed, or abused

Everyone has something in life that they just cannot let go. A pet peeve if you will. Well, in high school, there tends to be a lot of bullying and most of the time it goes unjustified. Moreover, I honestly cannot stand a person physically, mentally, or emotionally bringing another person down for his or her own selfish ego-boosts. It thoroughly disgusts me and gave me the edge I needed to do and say what I did when an innocent boy in my school was being pointlessly, harassed by the more "popular" group of boys.

For privacy purposes, I am going to change the victim's name to Tony. Tony was a good kid and a very good student. He did not bother anyone and kept to himself most of the time. It was not until one day during speech class that he had to talk about something he was interested in did the true emotional abuse begin. While giving his speech about fictional fantasy games, a boy from the football team threw a ball of paper at Tony and told him no one cares.

I do not know why this boy would say something like this in front of me, a senior who was acting as a teacher's

Appendix A: Additional Anger Stories

aide, nonetheless in front of the teacher, but what perhaps surprised me more was what the teacher did – Nothing. All I could think was, 'are you serious?' She merely shushed the boy. However, did that stop him? Of course it did not! He continued to be rude and disrespectful and still the teacher made little effort to subside the boy.

All I could think about was how wrong the whole situation was. How could a teacher not care that her pupil was being verbally attacked? Why would the other students find this boy's obnoxious insolence funny? Why provoke the boy's actions at Tony's expense? This all just got me furious that I completely lost all control of my right mind.

After about the third time he interrupted Tony and got his satisfying laughter, I could not help but intrude. I grabbed a piece of paper, balled it up, and threw it at the disrespectful juvenile and called him out on his horrible behavior. It went something like:

"Shut that annoying egotistical mouth of yours and learn to listen to someone smarter than you for once." The teacher told me to stop but I could not. "You have not earned a single good grade in your life, and I know, I correct your papers." By now the teacher is actually pushing me towards the door, but I kept going. "Do you get pleasure from Tony's pain? So you can throw a ball, big deal," I continued to say as I picked up another piece of paper and threw it at him. "In thirty years you will be working for minimum wage and this so called "nerd" will be your multi-millionaire boss."

The teacher was then shouting at me to leave, so I turned my attention towards her, "And you! What kind of teacher, no, human-being, just sits there while an innocent boy gets emotionally harassed?" She ignored my question and continued to get me out of her room. But, I was not satisfied. My anger was not released and this situation was not justified yet. "You know why school, even campus shootings occur? Because the teachers and students," I added turning my attention towards the class, "just sit there not doing anything, or worse, fueling the flame!"

By the terrified and guilty expressions on their faces, my anger quickly subsided, but the teacher was now infuriated with me. Knowing her place, she did not lose control however. "Sahar," she began in a stern aggravated voice, "leave now and go to the office." Honestly, I was already going to go that way, so I left.

On my way to the office, I had a feeling of guilt wash over me. There is no fact proven that any of them would have made Tony shoot up the school, and I really had no right to throw things at a younger student. I even felt a bit of panic wash over me. Was I going to get in serious trouble? I have never been in trouble. Never had detention, or anything of the sort, so I was terrified.

Now, I did not get in much trouble, but I did have to apologize for acting out and for throwing paper at a younger student. The teacher even apologized to Tony and the delinquent got proper punishment. I wish I could say I changed things, but I really do not know. I like to hope I did.

Maybe I only hope I did, so it will somehow justify my outrageous actions. An excuse I like to use for that is, 'sometimes it takes extreme measures to ensure that the horrific does not happen.' Which I completely agree with, but that old saying, 'Two wrongs don't make a right,' only contradict me.

With every action comes a consequence. Good or bad, they happen. My story, for example, is a perfect way to rid myself of that rage, because in my mind, I was righting a wrong. That is, until I took it too far and I became unforgivably guilty, but because I could not see my limit through the dark sheets of rage, I only started another fire, I began to make things worse instead of fixing them, which was the complete opposite of my means of action.

Looking back on it, it was like I was just watching myself and couldn't do anything to stop myself from stepping over that line. I became something ugly to myself because I could not sense my own interdependence.

Now don't get me wrong, everything I said I meant with everything I had at the time, there are just boundaries I know I should not have ignored. I supposed without feeling guilty afterwards though, I would not have been able to clear my conscience to get up the courage I needed to do what was right.

Jose's Anger Story: Lies & "Sabotage"

Core Emotional Issues

- 2. Being used, tricked, lied to, or deceived by someone
- 3. Disrespect toward you, a friend, or loved one
- 16. Passive or active "sabotage", delay, or blockage, by someone, of an idea, a solution, an objective, a task, a communication, or a project that is important to you

The part of my life that I most remember being angry about, happened to me last year. I had recently learned that I had a band concert on a Tuesday night that I was scheduled to work, so I decided to look around and find someone to work for me. I asked all of the people that I was friends with that worked with me and they all said that they were busy. I decided to ask one of the people that no one liked to work with to work for me. Before I was able to ask that person to work for me, a coworker named Devantia called and said that Miguel, another coworker who is a friend of mine, was going to work for me and that I shouldn't ask the other person.

When I talked to Miguel about it, he denied that he would work for me. Because he is my friend, I knew him and knew that he was joking and just trying to make me upset. It finally came down to fifteen minutes before he would have to be at work for me and I had lost my patience with him and told him that I knew he was going to work for me and that he could stop the game.

When he heard this he decided to actually not work for me, saying he had to do biology homework. I had to angrily call my place of employment and tell them that I would not be able to go to work because of having to play in a band concert. Fortunately, they said that it was okay. Even though they were okay with the fact that I couldn't come to work, I was very upset. I went to my band concert and when the choir started to sing, I looked into the audience and saw Miguel there, this made me absolutely irate. The fact that he lied to me and potentially could have gotten me fired just for his enjoyment, made me decide I had to get him back.

I decided that, that night I would buy window markers and black out all of the windows on his car. So, after the concert I went to Wal-Mart and bought the markers. Then at ten that night I went and blacked out all of his windows on his car. I then went home and got ready for bed. The next morning I went to school and saw Miguel. But, he did not seem very upset. I decided to ask his sister if he was actually upset or not and she said that he was very angry, and that she had never seen him that angry before.

Miguel and I never actually talked very much about what we each had done wrong, aside from joking about how angry we were at each other. Some of the core emotional issues that I felt that my friend had violated included being used by my friend, being disrespected, and being denied something important to me.

Ranesia's Anger Story: Harm to Family & Trust Violation

Core Emotional Issues

- 6. Violation of Trust
- 10. A friend, a loved one, a helpless person, or an innocent person being threatened, harmed, or abused

I've experienced anger many times and in many ways, but the most anger I have ever experienced towards anyone was toward my father. He put me and my family through more pain and emotions than I have ever felt in my entire life. And I had never felt sorrier for anyone then I did for my mom, who was the victim of his abuse.

About a year and a half ago my mom had started getting suspicions about my dad talking to a girl online on his computer at work. Credit card bills later showed that he had been sending her flowers for her birthday and greeting cards for other random holidays. My mom first tried to hide it from me and my brother because she did not want us knowing that anything was wrong, or have us worry. Once my brother and I found out we were both furious and had lost so much respect for my dad wondering how he could do this to our family. My mom even told me that she had gotten on to his email account and looked at conversations of theirs and they had conversations about us, which made me even more furious.

My dad doing this made me feel so used, like he did not even care about any of us. I just couldn't stop being mad at him. My mom finally made him stop talking to this girl online, and my dad said that he would be truthful. As time went on my mom and I started to trust my dad again, and then he started doing some really bad things. He committed adultery with my uncle's new wife and my mom found out. What my mom didn't know was that while my dad was talking to the girl online he was also talking to my aunt.

I just did not understand how my dad could do this. I went to sleep angry every night thinking that my dad did not love any of us. I did not know what to do anymore and I was always scared my mom was going to hurt herself. During that year I told my dad that I hated him for the first and last time. I would cry myself to sleep thinking that my parents were going to get a divorce and one of them was going to move away and I would not see them anymore. At one point after I found all of this out I thought about moving out of my house and never talking to my dad again, and sometimes even wished that they would get a divorce just because I was sick of it all. But I could not leave my mom in that situation.

After my mom changed my dad's passwords and my dad got a new job things finally started looking better for them. But my trust for my dad will never be the same again. He almost tore my family apart and made my mom miserable. My parents have now been married for 22 years, soon to be 23, and I know that there are many more years to come in their marriage, with many more opportunities for my dad to do what is right or create more sorrow.

Zixin's Anger: Emotional Abuse

Core Emotional issue

- **10. A friend, a loved one, a helpless person, or an innocent person being threatened, harmed, or abused**

At some point in our lives, each and every one of us experiences the loss of someone or something close to our hearts. The grief that follows it can be insufferable or sometimes impossible. Grief has five stages: Denial, anger, bargaining, depression, and lastly acceptance.

I attended high school in relatively small town in Georgia. During my senior year I faced a tragic loss of a good friend. I woke up on that Sunday morning just as I would any other day. I walked upstairs, planning to get a bite to eat for breakfast. As I reached the top of the stairs my mom and dad both looked at me as if something bad had happened.

The first thing my mom said was, "Zixin, have you heard anything about your friend Paul?" I thought to myself, what could she possibly be talking about? She told me that she got a phone call a few minutes ago from our neighbor, Mrs. Williams. She had told mom that the rumor this morning was that my friend Paul Wingfield had committed suicide in the middle of the football field at the high school. I lost my breath for a few seconds and my mind went ballistic. I had thoughts racing through my head wondering what, when, where, and why?

Appendix A: Additional Anger Stories

At first I did not want to believe it. How could this happen, it has happened to other people but how could it happen to me? In other words, I was denying this tragic situation.

I had left my cell phone at a friend's house the night before; hence, I had no way of knowing this had happened until I heard the horrible news from my parents. Immediately after finding this out, I grabbed my shoes, ran out the door, and drove to get my cell phone. I had a few missed calls and text messages from friends. I called my friend Carolyn back and asked if this was really true, and unfortunately the answer was yes. At this point I had no anger within me at all.

The only thing I could think is why? I started bawling as we left and headed over to Fred and Kristine's house, Paul's parents. We arrived and could hardly find a place to park. I went inside and saw several of my friends, some of their parents, Paul's brother and sister, and some of their other family members. Everyone was sobbing and all we could do is hug and share our sorrow and love for Paul.

After a few hours I thought why am I crying, this makes me furious. How could Paul do this to me, his family, friends, and the community? Did he not realize how much everyone loves and cares for him? Did he not think about how this would affect everyone? Paul had so many friends, so many people who adored him. Everyone loved being around him and he had great plans for the future. But they were all wasted.

I do not know how many times I said out loud to myself, "Paul I am so mad at you how or why could you do this?" I kept my anger inside for a long time; I chose not to talk about what had happened because all it would do was make me even more angry. Although this was not a healthy decision, it helped me to appear as a strong individual. I did not express my true feelings to people. I was stuck in the stage of anger for at least two months. In those two months I seemed to be in a bad mood all the time.

There were so many little things that would make me angry that were not worth getting mad over. For example, if something was planned earlier in the week and the plans fell through, I would get mad. I temporarily damaged relationships with my family, my friends, and my boyfriend.

Finally over time, I proceeded through the last stages of grief. This experience was and still is the hardest thing I have ever been through. Anger is a fact of life, although we may not like it, it is something we have to deal with as we go through life.

Ahmed's Anger: Disrespect, Trust Violation, Property Harm

Core Emotional Issues

- 3. Disrespect toward you, a friend, or loved one
- 6. Violation of Trust
- 11. Your property being carelessly or purposefully lost, damaged, or stolen

It took me a very long time to think of a time when I got really angry, because I don't get angry often. It happened three years ago when I was in my senior year of high school. It was in Grand Rapids, where I lived all of my early life. As a part of our high school spirit week, one day was Pajama Day. So, to participate, I wore my winter pajama bottoms, a favorite t-shirt and favorite slippers.

It was the end of my English class, so, with the rest of my class, I was exiting the room. While I was walking, Jason, a good friend of mine stepped on the back of one of my slippers (they were open-backed) and tore it all along the seam. That alone made me mad but the worst part was that he completely ignored what had happened and continued on walking. Later, when I confronted him about this, he just blew me off. And when I pressed the issue, and insisted that he would have to pay for my torn slippers, he thought I was joking. Even though I saw him a lot, I didn't talk to him for the rest of spirit week. I was really mad.

Of the core emotional issues, this falls under 3, 6, and mostly 11. Three, because I felt disrespected and I thought Jason was a better friend than that. I also felt slighted and let down. This experience mostly falls under the eleventh core emotional issue. I feel that Jason carelessly destroyed my property, i.e.: my slippers and I really like those slippers. The part that still gets me more than the actual property destruction though, is that he just didn't seem to care.

Before this incident, I felt relatively normal and happy. There was nothing that I remember that was bothering me that day so there was no anger already built up. I was a little peeved when my shoe got torn but the anger came when I was effortlessly blown off. Even worse, because my slipper was now torn, and my English class was my first class of the day, I had to walk around with that broken slipper all day. This reminded me of the incident, it festered in my mind. I brooded about it all day until I got home and was able to take them off, after which my anger subsided rather quickly.

The whole time during the short conflict, I wanted to MAKE Jason pay for the slipper (monetarily, not by my doing something bad to him to get revenge). And I even wanted to somehow sue him. Of course, I did not go through with this and we are in fact still good friends. Looking back, I think about how trivial this anger of mine was, and how I should have just let it go, but at that time I was furious. Even so, the conflict was swept under the rug by the weekend and there hasn't been any animosity between Jason and myself ever since. Yeah for happy endings!

Isaac's Anger: Emotional, Physical, and Property Abuse

Core Emotional Issues

- 3. **Disrespect toward you, a friend, or loved one**
- 9. **Being physically, verbally, financially, sexually, or emotionally abused, bullied or cheated**
- 10. **A friend, a loved one, a helpless person, or an innocent person being threatened, harmed, or abused**

I recently attended a small party of 20 with some real close friends. There was a young man there, Ed, who I consider my friend, but who is one of those people who just doesn't care what anyone thinks. He is one of the rudest individuals I've ever met. There has been several times when I asked myself why I even associate with this individual.

Back to my story, at this party we were all having a good time. We were just relaxing, but this friend of mine seemed to be trying to start something negative with someone. It seems that he had decided to turn most of his bad attention to my best friend, Nathan. My friend Nathan did not do anything to provoke or deserve any of this harassment from Ed. He wasn't physically harming Nathan, but some of the things he said to him were just terrible.

For the most part I'm a very calm, go with the flow sort of individual. But, watching Ed do this verbal emotional abuse to my best friend, made me absolutely furious. I just wanted to run up to him and knock him out. But I didn't. I cooled down and asked him to lay off Nathan a little. I thought that things were going to be okay, because he did what I had asked. Not even a half a hour later he was doing his negative verbal abuse to someone else. I said to myself, "I can't let him continue to do this." I decided to start giving him a taste of his own medicine. He did not like this, but he continued to do his bad behavior anyway. I didn't know what to do. I was furious, and I felt like I was about to snap.

Then it happened. I couldn't hold my anger in any longer. Ed started rummaging through my other friend's refrigerator, making a mess, eating any food he wanted. My friend who was the owner of the house wasn't happy with any of this. Ed just finished making this huge sandwich, and I lost all control of myself, and so I grabbed the sandwich and I gave it to the owner. I said "here I think this is yours." Ed then proceeded to punch me in the head. I felt this uncontrollable rage rush throughout my entire body. I couldn't do anything about it. I went right after him. And by the time we got pulled off of and away from each other there was a broken chair and a broken table.

I was kicked outside and once there I immediately cooled down and felt like the worst person in the world. Why did I let myself get so angry and let myself stoop that low. This wasn't me. The only thing I could do was say how sorry I was for everything. After a few days, I ended up making up with Ed. But still to this day I feel bad about losing all control of myself that night.

Isabella's Anger: Disrespect, Time Abuse, Wrongful Credit

Core Emotional Issues

- 3. Disrespect toward you, a friend, or loved one
- 6. Violation of Trust
- 8. Broken Promises
- 13. Someone wrongfully taking credit for your idea or achievement
- 16. Passive or active "sabotage", delay, or blockage, by someone, of an idea, a solution, an objective, a task, a communication, or a project that is important to you
- 17. Anything that you consider to be meaningfully unjust or unfair
- 19. Abuse of your time

    Anger is a common emotion that can lead to great insight about one's self or be an immense downfall, depending on how the emotion is handled. It can be another successfully climbed rock that leads a person closer to the summit, or the last stumbling block that leads to his or her demise. Most of all, it's a mirror of someone's true character. Anger can be sparked in an instant, at any time, place, or in this case, basement.

    The last quarter of my senior high school year had finally come and I intended to tackle any matter that would be thrown my way. Little did I know or anticipate what or who would cross my path. High school drama quickly ensued. I was enrolled in an astronomy class that was very involved but enjoyable. The final project counted for 60% of our grade. We were to hypothetically plan and build a space station that could sustain life out in space, and we would be working on this project in four member groups.

My group looked something like this: me; my best friend, Rachel; a mutual friend of ours, Ginger; and a "friend" that was equivalent to an acquaintance, Beth. All was well in our group work until Beth started showing signs of passive aggressiveness.

Four days before the project was due, we as a group decided to meet that night at Rachel's house at 5 and work until 11 o'clock. Rachel and I had been researching for days on the conversion of urine to water process and were highly exhausted on the whole subject matter. The idea of sitting at table in her basement and researching/writing for hours at a time made our heads spin, and to make the situation even tougher, another one of our friends had come home from college and was staying at Rachel's house for the night.

We quickly said our hellos to her and then went back to work. Ginger's graduation party was also that night and had lasted until 5, so we weren't surprised when we heard the door bell ring at 6 and saw Ginger standing uneasily on the doorstep. We of course understood that she would be late this night, and so with no negativity, we delegated the task of recording the daily life of the space dwellers to her. And she hurriedly started her research on it.

Low and behold, Beth showed up at 6:30, unprepared and totally clueless about the material we had already covered for our project. This aggravated me but I tried to look past it and progress on to more pressing issues, such as the completion of the project that was due in 4 days and that counted as 60% of my grade. Instead of working with us on our project, Beth busied herself reading emails and laughing about all the drama that was going on in the high school scene at that moment.

She was oblivious to the significant part that she played in the whole affair. After she gossiped for a few minutes, she proceeded to notify our group that she had to be at work at 7:30 and so would have to leave at 7:15 to get there on time. That gave us forty solid minutes to really put the pedal to the metal and get moving on the project, so I thought. But no, Beth would have none of that.

She started saying how we needed to be more creative and came up with an idea on how to save money in relation to the space shuttle. Her idea was that the space station dwellers would be teleported up into space station. At the time, I was so annoyed that I thought that I would rather have her gone so that she wouldn't be able to continue distracting me and the other two group members.

7:15 rolled around and Beth left. 11 o' clock came and Rachel, Ginger, and I were temporarily free from the topics of bone loss, microgravity, and waste recycling. At last when I was home, in my very comfortable bed, I received a text message from Beth that said, "U didnt tell me wut 2 research so im not going 2 do any 2nite". And that was the straw that broke the angry camel's back. I didn't answer that text nor did I confront her right away about it. That night, I went through the whole anger inspired speech that I was going to give to her the next day.

It went like this: "Beth. You haven't been at any of the meetings, given any valuable information to the group, or typed a single sentence about space. You are out of the group. Have fun figuring out the ratio of water each person needs per calorie that they expend out in space." Then I would walk away. When I did see her the following day, I was so angry that I couldn't even look at her.

The thought of being used and taken so lightly disgusted me. I didn't explode until the first word came out her mouth. That's when I said, "You have done nothing to help this project forward. We have done all the work and if you expect to present any of this information to the class on Wednesday, you will have to help carry the rest of the workload."

After getting my feelings and thoughts out, I felt elated. Yes I was still angry at letting it get that far but I was proud of speaking up for myself and my fellow group members. I didn't totally let go of that anger until we had pitched our plan to the class and received a final grade of "A" on the assignment.

After reviewing the "Twenty Core Emotional Issues that Stimulate or Trigger Anger," I found that at least 3 accurately pertained to this situation. I felt that the whole situation was very unfair. Three people were carrying Beth on their backs and she was going to get credit for project just the same. Second, we had invested time and commitment to the project while Beth took for granted our efforts. Third, I was afraid that she would end up getting full credit for work that I, Rachel, or Ginger had done.

The funny thing is, I just saw Beth at a Chinese restaurant last week and I still felt a tinge of bitterness towards her. Anger has a way with people. If it isn't dealt with properly, it has tremendous effects on peoples' outlooks on life and how they interact with other people. I come across anger events daily, but if I let those incidents bring me down and define me, I've admitted defeat and I refuse to let that happen.

Travon's Anger: Violation of Trust, Loved One Harmed

Core Emotional Issues

- 2. Being used, tricked, lied to, or deceived by someone
- 6. Violation of Trust
- 7. Abuse of Authority or Power
- 10. A friend, a loved one, a helpless person, or an innocent person being threatened, harmed, or abused

It was a typical day, something that was more normal than seeing the sun. It was just a simple day that our family would be traveling a seemingly long fifteen miles just to visit my oldest brother. I admired him so much.

The day seemed so short but yet exhausting, we arrived at his apartment around ten o'clock in the morning. The doors were locked, and the shades were shut, but his car was still in the small but identified spot. I remember looking through the edge of the window and seeing him sitting there against the wall, as though he was playing a trick on our mother, just to make her mad. At around eleven my aunt had contacted the landlord to open the door.

My emotions at this point were wild, I don't exactly remember what I was thinking but I do know it probably looked like I had been living on pixie sticks. The thrill of seeing my oldest brother brought joy to me; he was a role model, a hero, a best friend, and family. The key turned the lock to open, and before anyone could say hi I found myself standing at his bedroom doorway screaming as I stared at my dead brother.

My brother was diagnosed with acute Schizophrenia at a young age. It was controlled with medication until doctors decided maybe the disease just disappeared. Which as we all know, doesn't happen. Before consulting our family, his doctors, that had previously so carefully taken care of him all his life, had put the most dangerous tool in his hand, which he used to end his life.

As I was looking at him, all I thought was how selfish. How could he do this to me? How could he do this to our family, his friends, his girlfriend? How could he have done this? He had killed himself that morning due to acute Schizophrenia. His note apologized to everyone, saying that the voices told him it was the only way this would end things. It said the doctors told him he was okay, that the doctors promised him a normal life without medication.

I've never since in my life been so angry and disappointed. I was so very angry that my brother would choose to selfishly hurt all of our family members by killing himself. And, I had believed that those doctors we paid to put our lives in their hands would always do what is necessary to do what is right for us.

I was wrong; the doctors that had been taking care of him had been changing his drugs for long periods of time. They were conducting a study on him without his approval. I was very, very angry with them.

My deep anger about these things was fixed in place for many years. I wasn't really sure how to resolve my emotional issues in relation to this severe violation of trust by my brother and the doctors, but one day I finally realized that being angry would not ever bring my brother back. That maybe if I was to come to peace with the fact that he took his own life that maybe I'd be a happier person. I remember visiting his grave with flowers and tears and finally accepting his 'sorry' note that I had been angrily reliving and rejecting day after day since he died.

I now know that everything happens for a reason, even though we often do not understand, and that we react in our nature to situations in ways that we can handle at the time. I have forgiven what has happened, but in the back of my mind I feel as though I will never forget.

Daniel's Anger: Theft, Lies, Trust Violation

Core Emotional Issues

- **2. Being used, tricked, lied to, or deceived by someone**
- **3. Disrespect toward you, a friend, or loved one**
- **6. Violation of Trust**
- **11. Your property being carelessly or purposefully lost, damaged, or stolen**

"Bam!" I heard the noise come from upstairs. Frantically, I ran up the stairs to the living room where I found my nephew, Billy, crying because he had fallen, hitting his head on the coffee table while playing tag with his sister, Mandie. To get his mind off of how much his head hurt, I told him "If you don't stop crying, we might have to call an ambulance to come get you to perform surgery on your head!" Wide eyed and in disbelief, Billy stopped crying. When I told him that I was teasing, he smiled and felt a lot better. After I told them to settle down and watch T.V., I realized that I had abandoned my best friend, Jim, who was sitting in my basement, with his girlfriend, Tonie.

Before the upstairs commotion started, Jim, Tonie, and I were watching a funny movie. During the movie, Jim had asked me if he could borrow $20, until the next day when he got paid, so that he could put needed gas in his car and to get food for the two of them. I told them that I only had $100 that was my mom's for her prescription and some groceries. I told my friend that if I had any money left after purchasing those items, I will lend him that. He agreed to that, ending that conversation about money.

When I go back to my friends, they said that they had received a call and had to leave right away. I thought that something seemed weird about this. Best friends know each other very well. Since I have known Jim for twelve years, I feel that I know when something isn't right with him.

After Jim and Tonie left, I went to the drug store to take care of my responsibilities. While standing at the counter waiting to get my mother's prescription, I opened my wallet and saw that all of my money was gone. At that moment, I knew that Jim and Tonie had stolen my money. I remembered that they had watched me place the money in my wallet while I was watching the movie with them. They must have taken the money when I was upstairs. This stealing became even more distressing as all of my calls to Jim's phone went directly to his voice mail. He had turned off his phone and, because of that, I became furious!

The next day, after trying to reach Jim all night, I decided to stop by his house. When I got to the door, to my surprise, Tonie was outside talking to one of her friends named Donnie. Tonie's eyes widened when she saw me. "Where's Jim?" I stated coldly. She said "he's in his room, he just got up." As I walked inside and entered Jim's room, his head flew up as if he had just seen a ghost. The anger that I had built up over night was just beginning to be released as I literally shouted, "Where's my money?!"

At that moment both of our eyes fell on the pile of cash crumbled up on the desk next to the bed he was laying on, he said "I don't know what you're talking about!" Instantly, I snatched the money that was obviously mine, and I ran out of the door, past Tonie and her friend. I walked quickly across the uneven grass to my white, Ford Taurus. When my car door was almost closed, Tonie's skinny hand slipped in to the door jam, stopping the car door from closing. She screamed "Give me that money back, it's Jim's. He has to live off that until he gets paid next week."

At this point, I had caught Jim and Tonie in their lies. First, I knew they hadn't gotten Jim's paycheck yet. Second, they had thirty dollars total and Jim's paychecks were at least 2-3 hundred dollars every other week. Third, Jim didn't get paid until the next week; meaning they never had any intention of paying me back; had I lent them the twenty dollars that they had originally requested.

At that moment, all my anger erupted as I opened my car door, stood up, and made it very clear that I would not give them any money back and that I expected the other seventy dollars back as well. Then, Tonie started to threaten me, stating that she would get Jim to beat me up. To that I responded with "It wouldn't make a difference because you stole from me". I believed that with the adrenaline I had then, a fight would not have diminished my resolve. Tonie then screamed for Jim to come and beat me up.

My furor momentarily transformed to humor at her threats, so I cracked a joke saying, "Oh, you need you need Jim to help you be bad." Not even a second later, Jim pushed me into my car, almost knocking me down. That's when I jumped up and punched him in the face and he fell to the ground. He then ran back to the house yelling that he would get me back.

Luckily, my mom had the money to cover her prescription and pay for groceries. We were able to avoid involving the cops and, the best part was that, I got to punch Jim in the face. In the end, my mother's boyfriend, George, got Jim to pay me back every dime of my mother's money.

To this day, it still makes me angry to think that my best friend would steal from me and wreck our friendship over money; especially when he found out, three weeks later, that his girlfriend Tonie had stolen money numerous times. After that, Jim tried to patch up our friendship saying that Tonie was at fault for all of it, but clearly I knew, that he had stolen my mother's money and lied too.

To this day, Jim and I are not close friends, but I did forgive him because, I was taught as a child that, everyone deserves to be forgiven. I will never forget this conflict because it made me realize that trust is something that can be easily destroyed. The quote "Keep your friends close but your enemies closer," is a motto that I live by. Thanks to Jim and Tonie, I will probably have trust issues with my friends for the rest of my life, but, then again, I guess it's better to be safe than sorry.

www.ingramcontent.com/pod-product-compliance
Lightning Source LLC
Chambersburg PA
CBHW051924160426
43198CB00012B/2034